Poems and Songs Celebrating America

Edited by
ANN BRAYBROOKS

DOVER PUBLICATIONS, INC.
Mineola, New York

DOVER THRIFT EDITIONS

GENERAL EDITOR: MARY CAROLYN WALDREP

EDITOR OF THIS VOLUME: JANET B. KOPITO

ACKNOWLEDGMENTS: SEE PAGES IX–X.

Copyright

Copyright © 2014 by Dover Publications, Inc.
All rights reserved.

Bibliographical Note

Poems and Songs Celebrating America, first published by Dover Publications, Inc., in 2014, is a new anthology containing 121 poems and songs reprinted (with the exception of those listed in the Acknowledgments) from standard editions. Ann Braybrooks has made the selections and provided all of the introductory material.

Library of Congress Cataloging-in-Publication Data

Poems and Songs Celebrating America / edited by Ann Braybrooks.
    pages cm. — (Dover thrift editions)
Includes index.
  ISBN-13: 978-0-486-49881-2 (pbk)
  ISBN-10: 0-486-49881-6 (pbk)
 1. American poetry. 2. National songs—United States.
 3. United States—In literature. I. Braybrooks, Ann, editor.
  PS586.P54 2014
  811.008—dc23

2014014997

Manufactured in the United States by Courier Corporation
49881601   2014
www.doverpublications.com

Introduction to the Dover Edition

From Benjamin Franklin's "The Mother Country" to Julia Alvarez's "I, Too, Sing América"—as well as from the Revolutionary War period in the late 1700s to the inauguration in 2009 of the forty-fourth U.S. president, Barack Obama—the verses in this volume sing joyfully, purposefully, at times sentimentally, even bombastically, of America's origins, struggles, enormity, energy, and promise.

In addition to the battle cries, tributes, and elegies included here are poems praising the American democratic process (John Greenleaf Whittier's "The Poor Voter on Election Day" and Walt Whitman's "Election Day, November, 1884") and the red, white, and blue: Joseph Rodman Drake's "The American Flag" and Minna Irving's "Betsy's Battle Flag."

In the spirit of celebration, and a literal and figurative return to earth, a handful of poems trumpet the nation's natural beauty: the Niagara's "voice of thunder" and "deep anthem" (Lydia Howard Sigourney); the prairies that "stretch, in airy undulations, far away" (William Cullen Bryant); the Rockies, under a rising moon, where "a million firs stand tipped with lucent fire" (Ella Higginson), and Yosemite's "great granite castles" (Joaquin Miller).

For the most part, the poems and songs in this collection celebrate America rather than examine it. The authors and composers are unabashedly patriotic and enthusiastic, rather than subtle, anxious, or objective. More than one author dashed off lines in a rush of national feeling. Francis Scott Key composed "The Star-Spangled Banner" during the War of 1812 after spending a night aboard a ship on the Chesapeake Bay watching the British bombard Fort McHenry, an American stronghold. The next morning, when Key observed that the flag "was still there"—waving over the ramparts—he was overcome with emotion and began writing the song that would become the nation's official anthem (represented here by an 1814 sheet music version).

The view from the top of Pike's Peak, America's easternmost "fourteener"—a mountain that rises more than 14,000 feet above sea level—inspired Katharine Lee Bates, a Wellesley College professor who had traveled from the East Coast to Colorado in the summer of 1893, to write "America the Beautiful," evoking the "purple mountain majesties above the fruited plain."

In *An Autobiography in Brief,* Bates recalled:

We strangers celebrated the close of the session by a merry expedition to the top of Pike's Peak, making the ascent by the only method then available for people not vigorous enough to achieve the climb on foot nor adventurous enough for burro-riding. Prairie wagons, their tail-boards emblazoned with the traditional slogan, 'Pike's Peak or Bust,' were pulled by horses up to the halfway house, where the horses were relieved by mules. We were hoping for half an hour on the summit, but two of our party because so faint in the rarefied air that we were bundled into the wagons again and started on our downward plunge so speedily that our sojourn on the peak remains in memory hardly more than one ecstatic gaze. It was then and there, as I was looking out over the sea-like expanse of fertile country spreading away so far under those ample skies, that the opening lines of the hymn floated into my mind.

Shock and grief, far different feelings, followed the assassination of President Abraham Lincoln, perhaps the most esteemed and eulogized American. The number of tributes to Lincoln, written immediately after his death in 1865 and thereafter, could fill volumes. Among those works gathered here are William Cullen Bryant's "Abraham Lincoln" ("Oh, slow to smite and swift to spare/Gentle and merciful and just!"); excerpts from Walt Whitman's "When Lilacs Last in the Dooryard Bloom'd" ("O powerful western fallen star!"); Paul Laurence Dunbar's "Lincoln" ("And wrote thee down among her treasured few"); and two by Vachel Lindsay: "Lincoln" and "Abraham Lincoln Walks at Midnight."

Patriotic verse had its heyday from the period spanning the Revolution to the latter part of the nineteenth century, when wars played out on American soil and the nation was being established and secured. Patriotic verse, by its nature, is meant to rouse, rally, and unite: Its bold, declamatory language helped provoke separation from Great Britain, maintain independence during the War of 1812, and preserve the Union.

In broadsheets, newspapers, magazines, and books, poets chronicled the events of the day, including battle gains and losses ("Eutaw Springs" by Philip Freneau and "The Cumberland" by Henry Wadsworth Longfellow) and the deaths of heroes and leaders (Nathan Hale, George Washington, Abraham Lincoln, Frederick Douglass, William Lloyd

Garrison). The distribution of Oliver Wendell Holmes's poem "Old Ironsides" helped prevent the decommissioning of the U.S.S. *Constitution*, an eighteenth-century 44-gun Navy frigate that earned its nickname during service in the War of 1812. Slain Civil War soldiers were honored equally in "The Blue and the Gray" by Francis Miles Finch, who had discovered that the women of a Columbus, Mississippi, memorial association laid flowers on both Confederate and Union graves on Decoration Day, 1866:

> From the silence of sorrowful hours,
>   The desolate mourners go,
> Lovingly laden with flowers,
> Alike for the friend and the foe:—
>   Under the sod and the dew,
>   Waiting the Judgment-Day:—
>   Under the roses, the Blue;
>   Under the lilies, the Gray.

and in "An Ode for Decoration Day" by Henry Peterson:

> O gallant brothers of the generous South,
>   Foes for a day and brothers for all time!
> I charge you by the memories of our youth,
>   By Yorktown's field and Montezuma's clime,
> Hold our dead sacred—let them quietly rest
> In your unnumbered vales, where God thought best.
>   ★★★
> And ye, O Northmen! be ye not outdone
>   In generous thought and deed.
> We all do need forgiveness, every one:
>   And they that give shall find it in their need.
> Spare of your flowers to deck the stranger's grave,
>   Who died for a lost cause:—

American attitudes and literature changed during the twentieth century, when wars were fought overseas, and poets—influenced by the innovative work of Emily Dickinson and Walt Whitman—experimented with form and expounded on everything but national themes. A handful of composers wrote popular songs that galvanized the troops and energized American civilians, but for the most part, few poets wrote verse glorifying America. Those authors who did address the subject did so with less approbation than their predecessors; the rose-colored spectacles of the past gave way to the horn-rimmed glasses and contact lenses of the late twentieth century: With McCarthyism in the 1950s and the prolonged, unpopular Vietnam War (1955–1975), protest songs and verse filled airwaves, coffee houses, college dorms, and bookstores. Celebrating America became déclassé.

Only when nearly 3,000 Americans and citizens of other nations were killed during the attacks on the Twin Towers in New York City and the Pentagon and the downing of United Airlines Flight 93 on September 11, 2001, did patriotic verse experience a revival. In the days following the attack, huge numbers of Americans recorded their shock, anger, fear, grief, faith, and nationalism in poems looped across paper or pounded out on computer keyboards. Thousands of 9/11 poems appeared on the Internet. Both novice and experienced authors wrote, revised, posted, and published.

Modern and contemporary verse about America may be more accessible and palatable to many readers than traditional verses. Instead of tilting toward jingoism, recent verse tends to provide a more balanced, encompassing, multifaceted view. It freely takes America to task, with the ultimate goal of creating a better, just nation for every citizen. America the nation—not only American literature—is richer as a result of work composed by Langston Hughes ("I, Too" and "Let America Be America Again"), Woody Guthrie ("This Land Is Your Land"), Maya Angelou ("On the Pulse of Morning"), and Julia Alvarez ("I, Too, Sing América"), plus a host of others (including Native Americans) who contemplate America. For the full range of the American experience, I encourage readers to seek out additional voices.

It is my hope that readers will enjoy the poems and songs here both for their historical value and their expressions of joy, pride, and gratitude. Yes, some of the poems are triumphalist and simplistic and inexpert and politically incorrect. (A number were chosen for their popularity and importance, not their literary brilliance.) And no, you don't have to agree with all of the views expressed by the writers. Yet even the most cynical, fed-up, downtrodden reader may experience a quiet thrill while reading Henry Wadsworth Longfellow's "Paul Revere's Ride" (a primary-school staple, with its rousing first lines, "Listen, my children, and you shall hear/Of the midnight ride of Paul Revere") or Walt Whitman's famous, invigorating "list" poem:

I Hear America Singing

I hear America singing, the varied carols I hear,
Those of mechanics, each one singing his as it should be blithe
 and strong,
The carpenter singing his as he measures his plank or beam,
The mason singing his as he makes ready for work, or leaves off
 work,
The boatman singing what belongs to him in his boat, the deck-
 hand singing on the steamboat deck,
The shoemaker singing as he sits on his bench, the hatter singing
 as he stands,
The wood-cutter's song, the ploughboy's on his way in the morn-
 ing, or at noon intermission or at sundown,
The delicious singing of the mother, or of the young wife at work,
 or of the girl sewing or washing,
Each singing what belongs to him or her and to none else,
The day what belongs to the day—at night the party of young
 fellows, robust, friendly,
Singing with open mouths their strong melodious songs.

Acknowledgments

Lawrence Ferlinghetti: "I Am Waiting" by Lawrence Ferlinghetti from A CONEY ISLAND OF THE MIND, copyright © 1958 by Lawrence Ferlinghetti. Reprinted by permission of New Directions Publishing Corp.

Shirley Geok-lin Lim: "Learning to Love America" copyright © by Shirley Geok-lin Lim. First published in *What the Fortune Teller Didn't Say,* 1998.

Woody Guthrie: "This Land Is Your Land." Words and Music by Woody Guthrie. WGP/TRO-© Copyright 1956, 1958, 1970 and 1972 (copyrights renewed) Woody Guthrie Publications, Inc. & Ludlow Music, Inc., New York, NY, administered by Ludlow Music, Inc. Used by Permission.

Langston Hughes: "Daybreak in Alabama", "I, Too", "Let America Be America Again" from THE COLLECTED POEMS OF LANGSTON HUGHES by Langston Hughes, edited by Arnold Rampersad with David Roessel, Associate Editor, copyright © 1994 by the Estate of Langston Hughes. Used by permission of Alfred A. Knopf, a division of Random House, Inc.

Robinson Jeffers: "Shine, Perishing Republic," copyright © 1934 by Robinson Jeffers and renewed 1962 by Donnan Jeffers and Garth Jeffers; from THE SELECTED POETRY OF ROBINSON JEFFERS by Robinson Jeffers. Used by permission of Random House, an imprint of The Random House Publishing Group, a division of Random House LLC. All rights reserved.

Carl Sandburg: "Chicago," from *Chicago Poems,* NY: Henry Holt & Company, 1916, p.3; "Prairie," from *Poetry Magazine,* July 1918 (Poetry Foundation).

Carl Sandburg: Excerpt from "The People, Yes" from *The Complete Poems of Carl Sandburg, Revised and Expanded Edition.* Copyright © 1969, 1970 by Lilian Steichen Sandburg, Trustee. Reprinted by permission of Houghton Mifflin Harcourt Publishing Company. All rights reserved.

Myra Sklarew: "Monuments," reprinted with the permission of the author. The poet would like to acknowledge the musical work "Citypiece: D.C. Monuments," composed by Rob Kapilow for the Kennedy Center's bicentennial concert, where the poem "Monuments" was first presented.

Contents

Poems and Songs
Celebrating America

BENJAMIN FRANKLIN (1706–1790)

A prominent Founding Father, Franklin was an author, printer, publisher, postmaster, inventor, scientist, political theorist, and diplomat. He helped draft the Declaration of Independence and was one of its signers. The phrase "ye bad neighbors" in the second-to-last stanza of "The Mother Country" alludes to France.

The Mother Country

"We have an old mother that peevish is grown;
She snubs us like children that scarce walk alone;
She forgets we're grown up and have sense of our own;
    Which nobody can deny, deny,
        Which nobody can deny.

If we don't obey orders, whatever the case,
She frowns, and she chides, and she loses all patience,
and sometimes she hits us a slap in the face,
    Which nobody can deny, etc.

Her orders so odd are, we often suspect
That age has impaired her sound intellect;
But still an old mother should have due respect,
    Which nobody can deny, etc.

Let's bear with her humors as well as we can;
But why should we bear the abuse of her man?
When servants make mischief, they earn the rattan,
    Which nobody should deny, etc.

Know too, ye bad neighbors, who aim to divide
The sons from the mother, that still she's our pride;
And if ye attack her we're all of her side,
    Which nobody can deny, etc.

We'll join in her lawsuits, to baffle all those,
Who, to get what she has, will be often her foes;
For we know it must all be our own, when she goes,
   Which nobody can deny, deny
      Which nobody can deny."

JOHN DICKINSON (1732–1808)

Dickinson, a lawyer and politician who has been called the "Penman of the Revolution," wrote "The Liberty Song" in response to the Townshend Acts of 1767, which levied additional duties on the Colonies by the British. Dickinson's friend Arthur Lee contributed a few stanzas. The lyrics contain the first use of the phrase "By uniting we stand, by dividing we fall." Dickinson was a delegate from Pennsylvania in the Continental Congress and a signer of the United States Constitution.

The Liberty Song

Come join hand in hand, brave Americans all,
And rouse your bold hearts at fair Liberty's call;
No tyrannous acts, shall suppress your just claim,
Or stain with dishonor America's name.

Chorus:
In Freedom we're born, and in Freedom we'll live.
   Our purses are ready,
   Steady, friends, steady;
Not as slaves, but as Freemen our money we'll give.

Our worthy forefathers—let's give them a cheer—
To climates unknown did courageously steer;
Thro' oceans to deserts, for freedom they came,
And, dying, bequeath'd us their freedom and fame.

Chorus

Their generous bosoms all dangers despis'd,
So highly, so wisely, their birthrights they priz'd;
We'll keep what they gave, we will piously keep,
Nor frustrate their toils on the land or the deep.

Chorus

The Tree, their own hands had to Liberty rear'd;
They liv'd to behold growing strong and rever'd;
With transport then cried,—"Now our wishes we gain,
For our children shall gather the fruits of our pain."

Chorus

How sweet are the labors that freemen endure,
That they shall enjoy all the profit, secure,—
No more such sweet labors Americans know,
If Britons shall reap what Americans sow.

Chorus

Swarms of placemen and pensioners soon will appear,
Like locusts deforming the charms of the year:
Suns vainly will rise, showers vainly descend,
If we are to drudge for what others shall spend.

Chorus

Then join hand in hand brave Americans all,
By uniting we stand, by dividing we fall;
In so righteous a cause let us hope to succeed,
For Heaven approves of each generous deed.

Chorus

All ages shall speak with amaze and applause,
Of the courage we'll show in support of our laws;
To die we can bear,—but to serve we disdain,
For shame is to freemen more dreadful than pain.

Chorus

This bumper I crown for our sovereign's health,
And this for Britannia's glory and wealth;
That wealth, and that glory immortal may be,
If she is but just, and we are but free.

Chorus

THOMAS PAINE (1737–1809)

British-born Paine became an important force in the American Revolution with his fiery political writing, which included *Common Sense* and the "Crisis" papers. Songs such as "Liberty Tree" were cheaply printed as broadsheets and distributed throughout the Colonies, where they were sung at home and public gatherings.

Liberty Tree
I.

In a chariot of light, from the regions of day,
    The goddess of liberty came,
Ten thousand celestials directed the way,
    And hither conducted the dame.
A fair budding branch from the garden above,
    Where millions with millions agree,
She brought in her hand, as a pledge of her love,
    And the plant she named, *Liberty tree*.

II.

The celestial exotic struck deep in the ground,
    Like a native it flourish'd and bore:
The fame of its fruit drew the nations around,
    To seek out this peaceable shore.
Unmindful of names or distinctions they came,
    For freemen like brothers agree;
With one spirit endued, they one friendship pursued,
    And their temple was *Liberty tree*.

III.

Beneath this fair tree, like the patriarchs of old,
    Their bread in contentment they ate,
Unvex'd with the troubles of silver or gold,
    The cares of the grand and the great.
With timber and tar they Old England supplied,
    And supported her pow'r on the sea:
Her battles they fought, without getting a groat,
    For the honour of *Liberty tree*.

IV.

But hear, O ye swains ('tis a tale most profane),
 How all the tyrannical pow'rs,
King, Commons, and Lords, are uniting amain,
 To cut down this guardian of ours.
From the east to the west blow the trumpet to arms,
 Through the land let the sound of it flee:
Let the far and the near, all unite with a cheer,
 In defence of our *Liberty tree*.

JONATHAN MITCHELL SEWALL
(1745–1808)

Sewall was raised by his uncle, Stephen Sewall, Chief Justice of the Supreme
Court of Massachusetts. He became a lawyer in Portsmouth, New Hampshire,
and wrote patriotic poems and songs during the Revolution.

On Independence

Come all you brave soldiers, both valiant and free,
It's for Independence we all now agree;
Let us gird on our swords, and prepare to defend,
Our liberty, property, ourselves and our friends.

In a cause that's so righteous, come let us agree,
And from hostile invaders set America free,
The cause is so glorious we need not to fear,
But from merciless tyrants we'll set ourselves clear.

Heaven's blessing attending us, no tyrant shall say,
That Americans e'er to such monsters gave way,
But fighting we'll die in America's cause,
Before we'll submit to tyrannical laws.

George the Third, of Great Britain, no more shall he reign,
With unlimited sway o'er these free States again,
Lord North, nor old Bute, nor none of their clan,
Shall ever be honor'd by an American.

May Heaven's blessings descend on our United States,
And grant that the union may never abate;
May love, peace, and harmony, ever be found,
For to go hand in hand America round.

Upon our grand Congress may Heaven bestow,
Both wisdom and skill our good to pursue;
On Heaven alone dependent we'll be,
But from all earthly tyrants we mean to be free.

Unto our brave Generals may Heaven give skill,
Our armies to guide, and the sword for to wield,
May their hands taught to war, and their fingers to fight,
Be able to put British armies to flight.

And now, brave Americans, since it is so,
That we are independent, we'll have them to know,
That united we are, and united we'll be,
And from all British tyrants we'll try to keep free.

May Heaven smile on us in all our endeavors,
Safe guard our seaports, our towns, and our rivers,
Keep us from invaders by land and by sea,
And from all who'd deprive us of our liberty.

PHILIP FRENEAU (1752–1832)

Freneau was called "The Poet of the Revolution" by admirers and "that ras-
cal Freneau" by those who disliked his politics. (George Washington was one
such detractor.) Freneau joined the New Jersey militia in 1778 and was captured
by the British, an experience he wrote about in *The British Prison-Ship*. In
addition to being a writer and editor, Freneau was a sea captain.

Eutaw Springs 1781

At Eutaw Springs the valiant died:
    Their limbs with dust are covered o'er.
Weep on, ye springs, your tearful tide;
    How many heroes are no more!

If in this wreck of ruin they
   Can yet be thought to claim a tear,
O smite thy gentle breast, and say
   The friends of freedom slumber here!

Thou, who shalt trace this bloody plain,
   If goodness rules thy generous breast,
Sigh for the wasted rural reign;
   Sigh for the shepherds sunk to rest!

Stranger, their humble graves adorn;
   You too may fall, and ask a tear:
'T is not the beauty of the morn
   That proves the evening shall be clear.

They saw their injured country's woe,
   The flaming town, the wasted field;
Then rushed to meet the insulting foe;
   They took the spear—but left the shield.

Led by thy conquering standards, Greene,
   The Britons they compelled to fly:
None distant viewed the fatal plain,
   None grieved in such a cause to die—

But, like the Parthians famed of old,
   Who, flying, still their arrows threw,
These routed Britons, full as bold,
   Retreated, and retreating slew.

Now rest in peace our patriot band;
   Though far from nature's limits thrown,
We trust they find a happier land,
   A brighter Phoebus of their own.

On the British Invasion 1814

From France, desponding and betray'd,
From liberty in ruins laid,
Exulting Britain has display'd
   Her flag, again to invade us.

Her myrmidons, with murdering eye,
Across the broad Atlantic fly
Prepared again their strength to try,
   And strike our country's standard.

Lord Wellington's ten thousand slaves,
And thrice ten thousand, on the waves,
And thousands more of brags and braves
   Are under sail, and coming

To burn our towns, to seize our soil,
To change our laws, our country spoil,
And Madison to Elba's isle
   To send without redemption.

In Boston state they hope to find
A yankee host of kindred mind
To aid their arms, to rise and bind
   Their countrymen in shackles:

But no such thing—it will not do—
At least, not while a Jersey Blue
Is to the cause of freedom true,
   Or the bold Pennyslvanian.

A curse on England's frantic schemes!
Both mad and blind—her monarch dreams
Of crowns and kingdoms in these climes
   Where kings have had their sentence.

Though Washington has left our coast,
Yet other Washingtons we boast,
Who rise, instructed by his ghost,
   To punish all invaders.

Go where they will, where'er they land,
This pilfering, plundering, pirate band,
They liberty will find at hand
   To hurl them to perdition:

If in Virginia they appear
Their fate is fix'd, their doom is near,
Death in their front and hell their rear—
    So says the gallant buckskin.

All Carolina is prepared,
And Charleston doubly on her guard;
Where, once, sir Peter badly fared,
    So blasted by fort Moultrie.

If farther south they turn their views,
With veteran troops, or veteran crews,
The curse of heaven their march pursues
    To send them all a-packing:

The tallest mast that sails the wave,
The longest keel its waters lave,
Will bring them to an early grave
    On the shores of Pensacola.

Stanzas to the Memory of General Washington, Who Died December 14, 1799

Terra tegit, populus maeret, calum habet!

Departing with the closing age
    To virtue, worth, and freedom true,
The chief, the patriot, and the sage
    To Vernon bids his last adieu:
        To reap in some exalted sphere
        The just rewards of virtue here.

Thou, Washington, by heaven design'd
    To act a part in human things
That few have known among mankind,
    And far beyond the task of kings;
        We hail you now to heaven received,
        Your mighty task on earth achieved.

While sculpture and her sister arts,
   For thee their choicest wreaths prepare,
Fond gratitude her share imparts
    And begs thy bones for burial there;
      Where, near Virginia's northern bound
      Swells the vast pile on federal ground.

To call from their obscure abodes
   The Grecian chief, the Roman sage,
The kings, the heroes, and the gods
    Who flourish'd in time's earlier age,
      Would be to class them not with you,—
      Superior far, in every view.

Those ancients of ferocious mould,
   Blood their delight, and war their trade,
Their oaths profaned, their countries sold,
    And fetter'd nations prostrate laid;
      Could these, like you, assert their claim
      To honor and immortal fame?

Those monarchs, proud of pillaged spoils,
   With nations shackled in their train,
Returning from their desperate toils
    With trophies,— and their thousands slain;
      In all they did no traits are known
      Like those that honor'd Washington.

Who now will save our shores from harms,
   The task to him so long assign'd?
Who now will rouse our youth to arms
    Should war approach to curse mankind?
      Alas! no more the word you give,
      But in your precepts you survive.

Ah, gone! and none your place supply,
   Nor will your equal soon appear;
But that great name can only die
    When memory dwells no longer here,
      When man and all his systems must
      Dissolve, like you, and turn to dust.

TIMOTHY DWIGHT (1752–1817)

After graduating from Yale at the age of seventeen, Dwight became a tutor, a school principal, and a chaplain with the Continental Army. He later was a Massachusetts legislator and a pastor of a Congregational Church in Fairfield, Connecticut. He was the president of Yale from 1795 to 1817.

Columbia

Columbia, Columbia, to glory arise,
The queen of the world, and child of the skies!
Thy genius commands thee; with rapture behold,
While ages on ages thy splendours unfold.
Thy reign is the last, and the noblest of time,
Most fruitful thy soil, most inviting thy clime;
Let the crimes of the east ne'er encrimson thy name,
Be freedom, and science, and virtue, thy fame.

To conquest, and slaughter, let Europe aspire
Whelm nations in blood, and wrap cities in fire
Thy heroes the rights of mankind shall defend,
And triumph pursue them, and glory attend.
A world is thy realm: for a world be thy laws,
Enlarged as thine empire, and just as thy cause;
On Freedom's broad basis, that empire shall rise,
Extend with the main, and dissolve with the skies.

Fair science her gates to thy sons shall unbar,
And the east see thy morn hide the beams of her star.
New bards, and new sages, unrival'd shall soar
To fame unextinguish'd when time is no more;
To thee, the last refuge of virtue designed,
Shall fly from all nations the best of mankind;
Here, grateful to heaven, with transport shall bring
Their incense, more fragrant than odours of spring.

Nor less shall thy fair ones to glory ascend,
And genius and beauty in harmony blend;
The graces of form shall awake pure desire,
And the charms of the soul ever cherish the fire;

Their sweetness unmingled, their manners refined,
And virtue's bright image instamp'd on the mind,
With peace and soft rapture shall teach life to glow,
And light up a smile in the aspect of woe.

Thy fleets to all regions thy power shall display,
The nations admire, and the oceans obey;
Each shore to thy glory its tribute unfold,
And the east and the south yield their spices and gold.
As the day-spring unbounded, thy splendour shall flow,
And earth's little kingdoms before thee shall bow:
While the ensigns of union, in triumph unfurl'd,
Hush the tumult of war, and give peace to the world.

Thus, as down a lone valley, with cedars o'erspread,
From war's dread confusion I pensively stray'd—
The gloom from the face of fair heaven retired;
The winds ceased to murmur; the thunders expired;
Perfumes, as of Eden, flow'd sweetly along,
And a voice, as of angels, enchantingly sung:
"Columbia, Columbia, to glory arise,
The queen of the world, and the child of the skies."

PHILLIS WHEATLEY (1753–1784)

Wheatley was the first woman poet of African ancestry to achieve acclaim in the United States. At about age seven, she arrived in Boston aboard a slave ship and was purchased by John Wheatley as a servant for his wife, Susanna. Early on, the Wheatleys recognized Phillis's genius and began educating her alongside their children. She learned Greek and Latin, and her translation of a tale from Ovid made Boston academics take note. While her original poems were lauded, and some were printed and distributed, she was unable to publish a book in America. In 1773, *Poems on Various Subjects, Religious and Moral* was published in England.

To His Excellency General Washington

Celestial choir, enthron'd in realms of light,
Columbia's scenes of glorious toils I write.
While freedom's cause her anxious breast alarms,
She flashes dreadful in refulgent arms.

See mother earth her offspring's fate bemoan,
And nations gaze at scenes before unknown!
See the bright beams of heaven's revolving light
Involved in sorrows and the veil of night!

    The Goddess comes, she moves divinely fair,
Olive and laurel binds Her golden hair:
Wherever shines this native of the skies,
Unnumber'd charms and recent graces rise.

    Muse! Bow propitious while my pen relates
How pour Her armies through a thousand gates,
As when Eolus heaven's fair face deforms,
Enwrapp'd in tempest and a night of storms;
Astonish'd ocean feels the wild uproar,
The refluent surges beat the sounding shore;
Or think as leaves in Autumn's golden reign,
Such, and so many, moves the warrior's train.
In bright array they seek the work of war,
Where high unfurl'd the ensign waves in air.
Shall I to Washington their praise recite?
Enough thou know'st them in the fields of fright.
Thee, first in peace and honors—we demand
The grace and glory of thy martial band.
Fam'd for thy valour, for thy virtues more,
Hear every tongue thy guardian aid implore!

    One century scarce perform'd its destined round,
When Gallic powers Columbia's fury found;
And so may you, whoever dares disgrace
The land of freedom's heaven-defended race!
Fix'd are the eyes of nations on the scales,
For in their hopes Columbia's arm prevails.
Anon Britannia droops the pensive head,
While round increase the rising hills of dead.
Ah! Cruel blindness to Columbia's state!
Lament thy thirst of boundless power too late.

    Proceed, great chief, with virtue on thy side,
Thy ev'ry action let the Goddess guide.
A crown, a mansion, and a throne that shine,
With gold unfading, Washington! Be thine.

Liberty and Peace

LO! freedom comes. Th' prescient muse foretold,
All eyes th' accomplish'd prophecy behold:
Her port describ'd, "She moves divinely fair,
Olive and laurel bind her golden hair."
She, the bright progeny of Heaven, descends,
And every grace her sovereign step attends;
For now kind Heaven, indulgent to our prayer,
In smiling peace resolves the din of war.
Fix'd in Columbia her illustrious line,
And bids in thee her future councils shine.
To every realm her portals open'd wide,
Receives from each the full commercial tide.
Each art and science now with rising charms,
Th' expanding heart with emulation warms.
E'en great Britannia sees with dread surprize,
And from the dazzling splendor turns her eyes.
Britain, whose navies swept th' Atlantic o'er,
And thunder sent to every distant shore;
E'en thou, in manners cruel as thou art,
The sword resign'd, resume the friendly part.
For Galia's power espous'd Columbia's cause,
And new-born Rome shall give Britannia law,
Nor unremember'd in the grateful strain,
Shall princely Louis' friendly deeds remain;
The generous prince th' impending vengeance eye's,
Sees the fierce wrong, and to the rescue flies.
Perish that thirst of boundless power, that drew
On Albion's head the curse to tyrants due.
But thou appeas'd submit to Heaven's decree,
That bids this realm of freedom rival thee.
Now sheathe the sword that bade the brave atone
With guiltless blood for madness not their own.
Sent from th' enjoyment of their native shore,
Ill-fated—never to behold her more!
From every kingdom on Europa's coast
Throng'd various troops, their glory, strength and boast.
With heart-felt pity fair Hibernia saw
Columbia menac'd by the Tyrant's Law:
On hostile fields fraternal arms engage,

And mutual deaths, all dealt with mutual Rage;
The muse's ear hears mother earth deplore
Her ample surface smoak with kindred gore:
The hostile field destroys the social ties,
And ever-lasting slumber seals their eyes.
Columbia mourns, the haughty foes deride,
Her treasures plunder'd, and her towns destroy'd:
Witness how Charlestown's curling smoaks arise,
In sable columns to the clouded skies.
The ample dome, high-wrought with curious toil,
In one sad hour the savage troops despoil.
Descending peace and power of war confounds;
From every tongue celestial peace resounds:
As for the east th' illustrious king of day,
With rising radiance drives the shades away,
So freedom comes array'd with charms divine,
And in her train commerce and plenty shine.
Britannia owns her independent reign,
Hibernia, Scotia, and the Realms of Spain;
And great Germania's ample Coast admires
The generous spirit that Columbia fires.
Auspicious Heaven shall fill with fav'ring gales,
Where e'er Columbia spreads her swelling sails:
To every realm shall peace her charms display,
And Heavenly freedom spread her golden ray.

To the Right Honourable William, Earl of Dartmouth, His Majesty's Principal Secretary of State for North America, &c.

Hail, happy day, when, smiling like the morn,
Fair Freedom rose New-England to adorn:
The northern clime beneath her genial ray,
Dartmouth, congratulates thy blissful sway:
Elate with hope her race no longer mourns,
Each soul expands, each grateful bosom burns,
While in thine hand with pleasure we behold
The silken reins, and Freedom's charms unfold.
Long lost to realms beneath the northern skies
She shines supreme, while hated faction dies:

Soon as appeared the Goddess long desired,
Sick at the view, she languished and expired;
Thus from the splendors of the morning light
The owl in sadness seeks the caves of night.

No more, America, in mournful strain
Of wrongs, and grievance unredressed complain;
No longer shalt thou dread the iron chain,
Which wanton Tyranny with lawless hand
Had made, and with it meant t' enslave the land.

Should you, my lord, while you peruse my song,
Wonder from whence my love of Freedom sprung,
Whence flow these wishes for the common good,
By feeling hearts alone best understood,
I, young in life, by seeming cruel fate
Was snatch'd from Afric's fancied happy seat:
What pangs excruciating must molest,
What sorrows labour in my parent's breast?
Steeled was that soul and by no misery moved,
That from a father seized his babe beloved:
Such, such my case. And can I then but pray
Others may never feel tyrannic sway?

For favours past, great Sir, our thanks are due,
And thee we ask thy favours to renew,
Since in thy power, as in thy will before,
To soothe the griefs, which thou did'st once deplore.
May heavenly grace the sacred sanction give
To all thy works, and thou for ever live
Not only on the wings of fleeting Fame,
Though praise immortal crowns the patriot's name,
But to conduct to heavens refulgent fane,
May fiery coursers sweep th' ethereal plain,
And bear thee upwards to that blest abode,
Where, like the prophet, thou shalt find thy God.

JOEL BARLOW (1754–1812)

Barlow was a chaplain in the Revolutionary Army, a member of the Hartford
Wits (a patriotic-minded literary group), an attorney, and a diplomat whose
duties took him to North Africa, Europe, and also England, where he became
friends with Thomas Paine. Barlow died of exposure in Poland after getting
caught up in Napoleon's retreat from Russia.

Excerpt from "The Columbiad (Book IV)"

　　Sun of the moral world! effulgent source
Of man's best wisdom and his steadiest force,
Soul-searching Freedom! here assume thy stand,
And radiate hence to every distant land;
Point out and prove how all the scenes of strife,
The shock of states, the impassion'd broils of life,
Spring from unequal sway; and how they fly
Before the splendor of thy peaceful eye;
Unfold at last the genuine social plan,
The mind's full scope, the dignity of man,
Bold nature bursting thro' her long disguise,
And nations daring to be just and wise.
　　Yes! righteous Freedom, heaven and earth and sea
Yield or withhold their various gifts for thee;
Protected Industry beneath thy reign
Leads all the virtues in her filial train;
Courageous Probity with brow serene,
And Temperance calm presents her placid mien;
Contentment, Moderation, Labor, Art,
Mould the new man and humanize his heart:
To public plenty private ease dilates,
Domestic peace to harmony of states.
Protected Industry, careering far,
Detects the cause and cures the rage of war,
And sweeps, with forceful arm, to their last graves,
Kings from the earth and pirates from the waves.

EDWARD BANGS (1756–1818)

Bangs, who became an attorney after graduating from Harvard in 1777, is just one of the many individuals who have been given credit for writing "Yankee Doodle." A different, shorter version is the state anthem of Connecticut.

Yankee Doodle

FATHER and I went down to camp,
 Along with Captain Gooding,
And there we see the men and boys,
 As thick as hasty pudding.

Chorus:
Yankee Doodle, keep it up,
 Yankee Doodle, dandy,
Mind the music and the step,
 And with the girls be handy.

And there we see a thousand men,
 As rich as 'Squire David;
And what they wasted every day
 I wish it could be savèd.

Chorus

The 'lasses they eat every day
 Would keep our house a winter;
They have so much that, I'll be bound,
 They eat whene'er they're a mind to.

Chorus

And there we see a swamping gun,
 As big as a log of maple,
Upon a deucèd little cart,
 A load for father's cattle.

Chorus

And every time they shoot it off,
 It takes a horn of power,
And makes a noise like father's gun,
 Only a nation louder.

Chorus

I went as nigh to one myself
   As Siah's underpinning;
And father went as nigh again,
   I thought the deuce was in him.

Chorus

Cousin Simon grew so bold,
   I thought he would have cocked it;
It scared me so, I shrinked if off,
   And hung by father's pocket.

Chorus

And Captain Davis had a gun,
   He kind of clapped his hand on't,
And stuck a crooked stabbing-iron
   Upon the little end on't.

Chorus

And there I see a pumpkin shell
   As big as mother's basin;
And every time they touched it off,
   They scampered like the nation.

Chorus

I see a little barrel, too,
   The heads were made of leather,
They knocked upon 't with little clubs
   To call the folks together.

Chorus

And there was Captain Washington,
   And gentlefolks about him,
They say he's grown so tarnal proud
   He will not ride without 'em.

Chorus

He had got on his meeting clothes,
   And rode a strapping stallion,
And gave his orders to the men,—
   I guess there was a million.

Chorus

The flaming ribbons in his hat,
   They looked so tearing fine ah,
I wanted peskily to get,
   To give to my Jemima.

Chorus

And then I see a snarl of men
   A digging graves, they told me.
So tarnal long, so tarnal deep,
   They 'tended they should hold me.

Chorus

It scared me so, I hooked it off,
   Nor stopped, as I remember,
Nor turned about, till I got home,
   Locked up in mother's chamber.

WILLIAM JAY (1769–1853)

An English nonconformist minister, Jay preached at Argyle Chapel in Bath
for over sixty years. Following his revivalist, populist convictions, he preached
to anyone who would listen, regardless of social rank or religious denomina-
tion. His grandson, William Jay Bolton, was a self-taught artist who designed
and created the first figural stained glass in the United States.

Mount Vernon

THERE dwelt the Man, the flower of human kind,
Whose visage mild bespoke his noble mind;
There dwelt the Soldier, who his sword ne'er drew
But in a righteous cause, to Freedom true;

There dwelt the Hero, who ne'er fought for fame,
Yet gained more glory than a Caesar's name;
There dwelt the Statesman, who devoid of art,
Gave soundest counsels from an upright heart;
And oh, Columbia, by thy sons caressed,
There dwelt the Father of the realms he blessed,
Who no wish felt to make his mighty praise,
Like other chiefs, the means himself to raise;
But there retiring, breathed in pure renown,
And felt a grandeur that disdained a crown.

JOSEPH HOPKINSON (1770–1842)

Hopkinson, son of Revolutionary War patriot Francis Hopkinson, was a member of the U.S. House of Representatives and later a judge for the U.S. District Court for the Eastern District of Pennsylvania. In 1798, Hopkinson wrote the lyrics to "Hail, Columbia," which had been composed by Philip Phile almost a decade earlier in honor of the first inauguration of George Washington. "Hail, Columbia" became one of the unofficial anthems of the United States until "The Star-Spangled Banner" was given the official title in 1931. The song is now the entrance march for the Vice President of the United States.

Hail, Columbia

Hail, Columbia! happy land!
Hail, ye heroes! heaven-born band!
   Who fought and bled in Freedom's cause;
   Who fought and bled in Freedom's cause,
And when the storm of war was gone,
Enjoy'd the peace your valor won.
   Let independence be your boast,
   Ever mindful what it cost;
   Ever grateful for the prize,
   Let its altar reach the skies.

Chorus:
Firm, united, let us be,
Rallying round our Liberty;
As a band of brothers join'd,
Peace and safety we shall find.

Immortal patriots! rise once more!
Defend your rights, defend your shore;
   Let no rude foe, with impious hand,
   Let no rude foe, with impious hand,
Invade the shrine where sacred lies
Of toil and blood the well-earn'd prize;
   While offering peace, sincere and just,
   In Heaven we place a manly trust,
   That truth and justice will prevail,
   And every scheme of bondage fail.

Chorus

Sound, sound the trump of fame!
Let WASHINGTON'S great name
   Ring thro' the world with loud applause,
   Ring thro' the world with loud applause:
Let every clime to freedom dear
Listen with a joyful ear.
   With equal skill, and godlike power,
   He govern'd in the fearful hour
   Of horrid war, or guides with ease
   The happier time of honest peace.

Chorus

Behold the chief who now commands,
Once more to serve his country stands—
   The rock on which the storm will beat,
   The rock on which the storm will beat:
But arm'd in virtue, firm and true,
His hopes are fix'd on Heaven and you.
   When Hope was sinking in dismay,
   When glooms obscured Columbia's day,
   His steady mind, from changes free,
   Resolved on death or Liberty.

Chorus

FRANCIS SCOTT KEY (1779–1843)

In September of 1814, during the War of 1812, from aboard a ship in the Chesapeake Bay, lawyer and amateur poet Key witnessed the nighttime bombardment of Fort McHenry by the British. The next morning, he saw the American flag still flying and was moved to write "Defence of Fort M'Henry," which became known as "The Star-Spangled Banner."

The Star-Spangled Banner

O! say, can you see, by the dawn's early light,
What so proudly we hail'd at the twilight's last gleaming,
Whose broad stripes and bright stars, thro' the perilous fight,
O'er the ramparts we watch'd, were so gallantly streaming.
And the rockets' red glare, the bombs bursting in air,
Gave proof through the night that our flag was still there;
O! say, does that star-spangled banner yet wave,
O'er the land of the free, and the home of the brave.

On the shore dimly seen through the mists of the deep,
Where the foe's haughty host in dread silence reposes;
What is that which the breeze, o'er the towering steep,
As it fitfully blows, half conceals, half discloses?
Now it catches the gleam of the morning's first beam;
In full glory reflected now shines in the stream.
'Tis the star-spangled banner; O! long may it wave,
O'er the land of the free, and the home of the brave.

And where is that band who so vauntingly swore,
That the havoc of war and the battle's confusion,
A home and a country, shall leave us no more?
Their blood has wash'd out their foul footsteps' pollution.
No refuge could save the hireling and slave,
From the terror of flight or the gloom of the grave.
And the star-spangled banner, in triumph doth wave,
O'er the land of the free, and the home of the brave.

O! thus be it ever when freemen shall stand
Between their lov'd home, and the war's desolation,
Blest with vict'ry and peace, may the Heav'n rescued land,
Praise the Pow'r that hath made and preserv'd us a nation!

Then conquer we must, when our cause it is just,
And this be our motto, "In God is our Trust";
And the star-spangled banner, in triumph shall wave
O'er the land of the free, and the home of the brave.

LYDIA HOWARD SIGOURNEY (1791–1865)

The "sweet singer of Hartford" was one of the first American women to have a prosperous literary career. She wrote more than sixty books and a thousand articles, and her fame extended to Europe. Her autobiography, *Letters of Life,* was released a year after her death.

Excerpt from "Indian Names"

YE say they all have pass'd away—
    That noble race and brave;
That their light canoes have vanish'd
    From off the crested wave;
That 'mid the forests where they roam'd,
    There rings no hunter's shout:
But their name is on your waters,
    Ye may not wash it out.

'T is where Ontario's billow
    Like ocean's surge is curl'd,
Where strong Niagara's thunders wake
    The echo of the world,
Where red Missouri bringeth
    Rich tribute from the West,
And Rappahannock sweetly sleeps
    On green Virginia's breast.

Ye say their conelike cabins,
    That cluster'd o'er the vale,
Have fled away like withered leaves
    Before the autumn gale;

But their memory liveth on your hills,
    Their baptism on your shore,
Your everlasting rivers speak
    Their dialect of yore.

Old Massachusetts wears it
    Upon her lordly crown,
And broad Ohio bears it
    Amid his young renown;
Connecticut hath wreath'd it
    Where her quiet foliage waves,
And bold Kentucky breathes it hoarse
    Through all her ancient caves.

Wachuset hides its lingering voice
    Within his rocky heart,
And Alleghany graves its tone
    Throughout his lofty chart.
Monadnock on his forehead hoar
    Doth seal the sacred trust:
Your mountains build their monument,
    Though ye destroy their dust.

Niagara

FLOW on forever, in thy glorious robe
Of terror and of beauty—God hath set
His rainbow on thy forehead, and the cloud
Mantled around thy feet.—Ad he doth give
Thy voice of thunder power to speak of him
Eternally—bidding the lip of man
Keep silence, and upon thy rocky altar pour
Incense of awe-struck praise.

    And who can dare
To lift the insect trump of earthly hope,
Or love, or sorrow,—'mid the peal sublime
Of thy tremendous hymn?—Even Ocean shrinks
Back from thy brotherhood, and his wild waves

Retire abashed.—For he doth sometimes seem
To sleep like a spent laborer, and recall
His wearied billows from their vexing play,
And lull them to a cradle calm:—but thou,
With everlasting, undecaying tide,
Dost rest not night or day.

   The morning stars,
When first they sang o'er young creation's birth,
Heard thy deep anthem,—and those wrecking fires
That wait the Archangel's signal to dissolve
The solid earth, shall find Jehovah's name
Graven, as with a thousand diamond spears,
On thine unfathomed page.—Each leafy bough
That lifts itself within thy proud domain,
Doth gather greenness from thy living spray,
And tremble at the baptism.—Lo! yon birds
Do venture boldly near, bathing their wing
Amid thy foam and mist—'Tis meet for them
To touch thy garment's hem,—or lightly stir
The snowy leaflets of thy vapor wreath,—
Who sport unharmed upon the fleecy cloud,
And listen at the echoing gate of heaven,
Without reproof. But as for us,—it seems
Scarce lawful with our broken tones to speak
Familiarly of thee.—Methinks, to tint
Thy glorious features with our pencil's point,
Or woo thee to the tablet of a song,
Were profanation.

   Thou dost make the soul
A wondering witness of thy majesty;
And while it rushes with delirious joy
To tread thy vestibule, dost chain its step,
And check its rapture with the humbling view
Of its own nothingness, bidding it stand
In the dread presence of the Invisible,
As if to answer to its God through thee.

WILLIAM CULLEN BRYANT (1794–1878)

For fifty years, Bryant was the Editor-in-Chief of the *New York Evening Post*, a position that made him a fortune and allowed him to exert considerable power in politics. It was Bryant who introduced candidate Abraham Lincoln at New York's Cooper Union, where Lincoln made a speech that helped him secure the Republican nomination and ultimately the Presidency.

Abraham Lincoln

Oh, slow to smite and swift to spare,
    Gentle and merciful and just!
Who, in the fear of God, didst bear
    The sword of power—a nation's trust.

In sorrow by thy bier we stand,
    Amid the awe that hushes all,
And speak the anguish of a land
    That shook with horror at thy fall.

Thy task is done—the bond are free;
    We bear thee to an honored grave,
Whose noblest monument shall be
    The broken fetters of the slave.

Pure was thy life; its bloody close
    Hath placed thee with the sons of light,
Among the noble host of those
    Who perished in the cause of right.

Oh Mother of a Mighty Race

Oh mother of a mighty race,
Yet lovely in thy youthful grace!
The elder dames, thy haughty peers,
Admire and hate thy blooming years.
    With words of shame
And taunts of scorn they join thy name.

For on thy cheeks the glow is spread
That tints thy morning hills with red;
They step—the wild deer's rustling feet,
Within thy woods are not more fleet;
   Thy hopeful eye
Is bright as thine own sunny sky.

Aye, let them rail—those haughty ones,
While safe thou dwellest with thy sons.
They do not know how loved thou art,
How many a fond and fearless heart
   Would rise to throw
Its life between thee and the foe.

They know not, in their hate and pride,
What virtues with thy children bide;
How true, how good, thy graceful maids
Make bright, like flowers, the valley shades;
   What generous men
Spring, like thine oaks, by hill and glen.

What cordial welcomes greet the guest
By thy lone rivers of the West;
How faith is kept, and truth revered,
And man is loved, and God is feared,
   In woodland homes,
And where the ocean border foams.

There's freedom at thy gates and rest
For Earth's down-trodden and opprest,
A shelter for the hunted head,
For the starved laborer toil and bread.
   Power, at thy bounds,
Stops and calls back his baffled hounds.

Oh, fair young mother! on thy brow
Shall sit a nobler grace than now.
Deep in the brightness of thy skies,
The thronging years in glory rise,
   And, as they fleet,
Drop strength and riches at thy feet.

Thine eye, with every coming hour,
Shall brighten, and thy form shall tower;
And when thy sisters, elder born,
Would brand thy name with words of scorn,
   Before thine eye,
Upon their lips the taunt shall die.

The Prairies

These are the gardens of the Desert, these
The unshorn fields, boundless and beautiful,
For which the speech of England has no name—
The Prairies. I behold them for the first,
And my heart swells, while the dilated sight
Takes in the encircling vastness. Lo! they stretch
In airy undulations, far away,
As if the ocean, in his gentlest swell,
Stood still, with all his rounded billows fixed,
And motionless forever. —Motionless?—
No—they are all unchained again. The clouds
Sweep over with their shadows, and, beneath,
The surface rolls and fluctuates to the eye;
Dark hollows seem to glide along and chase
The sunny ridges. Breezes of the South!
Who toss the golden and the flame-like flowers,
And pass the prairie-hawk that, poised on high,
Flaps his broad wings, yet moves not—ye have played
Among the palms of Mexico and vines
Of Texas, and have crisped the limpid brooks
That from the fountains of Sonora glide
Into the calm Pacific—have ye fanned
A nobler or a lovelier scene than this?
Man hath no part in all this glorious work:
The hand that built the firmament hath heaved
And smoothed these verdant swells, and sown their slopes
With herbage, planted them with island groves,
And hedged them round with forests. Fitting floor
For this magnificent temple of the sky—
With flowers whose glory and whose multitude

Rival the constellations! The great heavens
Seem to stoop down upon the scene in love,—
A nearer vault, and of a tenderer blue,
Than that which bends above our eastern hills.

As o'er the verdant waste I guide my steed,
Among the high rank grass that sweeps his sides
The hollow beating of his footstep seems
A sacrilegious sound. I think of those
Upon whose rest he tramples. Are they here—
The dead of other days?—and did the dust
Of these fair solitudes once stir with life
And burn with passion? Let the mighty mounds
That overlook the rivers, or that rise
In the dim forest crowded with old oaks,
Answer. A race, that long has passed away,
Built them;—a disciplined and populous race
Heaped with long toil, the earth, while yet the Greek
Was hewing the Pentelicus to forms
Of symmetry, and rearing on its rock
The glittering Parthenon. These ample fields
Nourished their harvests, here their herds were fed,
When haply by their stalls the bison lowed,
And bowed his maned shoulder to the yoke.
All day this desert murmured with their toils,
Till twilight blushed, and lovers walked, and wooed
In a forgotten language, and old tunes,
From instruments of unremembered form,
Gave the soft winds a voice. The red man came—
The roaming hunter tribes, warlike and fierce,
And the mound-builders vanished from the earth.
The solitude of centuries untold
Has settled where they dwelt. The prairie-wolf
Hunts in their meadows, and his fresh-dug den
Yawns by my path. The gopher mines the ground
Where stood their swarming cities. All is gone;
All—save the piles of earth that hold their bones,
The platforms where they worshipped unknown gods,
The barriers which they builded from the soil
To keep the foe at bay—till o'er the walls
The wild beleaguerers broke, and, one by one,

The strongholds of the plain were forced, and heaped
With corpses. The brown vultures of the wood
Flocked to those vast uncovered sepulchres,
And sat, unscared and silent, at their feast.
Haply some solitary fugitive,
Lurking in marsh and forest, till the sense
Of desolation and of fear became
Bitterer than death, yielded himself to die.
Man's better nature triumphed then. Kind words
Welcomed and soothed him; the rude conquerors
Seated the captive with their chiefs; he chose
A bride among their maidens, and at length
Seemed to forget,—yet ne'er forgot,—the wife
Of his first love, and her sweet little ones,
Butchered, amid their shrieks, with all his race.

Thus change the forms of being. Thus arise
Races of living things, glorious in strength,
And perish, as the quickening breath of God
Fills them, or is withdrawn. The red man, too,
Has left the blooming wilds he ranged so long,
And, nearer to the Rocky Mountains, sought
A wilder hunting-ground. The beaver builds
No longer by these streams, but far away,
On waters whose blue surface ne'er gave back
The white man's face—among Missouri's springs,
And pools whose issues swell the Oregon,
He rears his little Venice. In these plains
The bison feeds no more. Twice twenty leagues
Beyond remotest smoke of hunter's camp,
Roams the majestic brute, in herds that shake
The earth with thundering steps—yet here I meet
His ancient footprints stamped beside the pool.

Still this great solitude is quick with life.
Myriads of insects, gaudy as the flowers
They flutter over, gentle quadrupeds,
And birds, that scarce have learned the fear of man,
Are here, and sliding reptiles of the ground,
Startlingly beautiful. The graceful deer
Bounds to the wood at my approach. The bee,

A more adventurous colonist than man,
With whom he came across the eastern deep,
Fills the savannas with his murmurings,
And hides his sweets, as in the golden age,
Within the hollow oak. I listen long
To his domestic hum, and think I hear
The sound of that advancing multitude
Which soon shall fill these deserts. From the ground
Comes up the laugh of children, the soft voice
Of maidens, and the sweet and solemn hymn
Of Sabbath worshippers. The low of herds
Blends with the rustling of the heavy grain
Over the dark-brown furrows. All at once
A fresher wind sweeps by, and breaks my dream,
And I am in the wilderness alone.

JOSEPH RODMAN DRAKE (1795–1820)

While a medical student, Drake became friends with poet Fitz-Greene Halleck, and the two began collaborating on topical satirical verses that were published under a pseudonym in the *New York Evening Post*. When Drake died at twenty-five, his wife ignored his request that his unpublished poems be destroyed; the work was published fifteen years later with the assistance of his daughter. "The American Flag" was set to music by Antonin Dvořák in his Cantata, Opus 102.

The American Flag

When Freedom from her mountain height
    Unfurled her standard to the air,
She tore the azure robe of night,
    And set the stars of glory there;
She mingled with its gorgeous dyes
The milky baldric of the skies,
And striped its pure celestial white
With streakings of the morning light;
Then from his mansion in the sun
She called her eagle bearer down,
And gave into his mighty hand
The symbol of her chosen land.

Majestic monarch of the cloud,
   Who rear'st aloft thy regal form,
To hear the tempest trumpings loud
And see the lightning lances driven,
   When strive the warriors of the storm,
And rolls the thunder-drum of heaven
Child of the sun! to thee 'tis given
   To guard the banner of the free,
To hover in the sulphur smoke,
To ward away the battle stroke,
And bid its blendings shine afar,
Like rainbows on the cloud of war,
   The harbingers of victory!

Flag of the brave! thy folds shall fly,
The sign of hope and triumph high,
When speaks the signal trumpet tone,
And the long line comes gleaming on;
Ere yet the life-blood, warm and wet,
Has dimmed the glistening bayonet,
Each soldier eye shall brightly turn
To where thy sky-born glories burn,
And, as his springing steps advance,
Catch war and vengeance from the glance;
And when the cannon-mouthings loud
Heave in wild wreaths the battle shroud
And gory sabers rise and fall
Like shoots of flame on midnight's pall;
Then shall thy meteor glances glow,
   And cowering foes shall shrink beneath
Each gallant arm that strikes below
   That lovely messenger of death.

Flag of the seas! on ocean wave
Thy stars shall glitter o'er the brave;
When death, careering on the gale,
Sweeps darkly round the bellied sail,
And frighted waves rush wildly back
Before the broadside's reeling rack,

Each dying wanderer of the sea
Shall look at once to heaven and thee,
And smile to see thy splendors fly
In triumph o'er his closing eye.

Flag of the free heart's hope and home!
    By angel hands to valor given;
Thy stars have lit the welkin dome,
    And all thy hues were born in heaven.
Forever float that standard sheet!
    Where breathes the foe but falls before us,
With Freedom's soil beneath our feet,
    And Freedom's banner streaming o'er us?

AMOS BRONSON ALCOTT (1799–1888)

A teacher, lecturer, philosopher and author, Amos Bronson Alcott was the father of Louisa May Alcott, who incorporated family members and experiences into her novel, *Little Women*. Alcott was an abolitionist and advocate for women's rights and, with his friend Ralph Waldo Emerson, a member of the Transcendentalist movement in Massachusetts.

Garrison

FREEDOM'S first champion in our fettered land!
Nor politician nor base citizen
Could gibbet thee, nor silence, nor withstand.
Thy trenchant and emancipating pen
The patriot Lincoln snatched with steady hand,
Writing his name and thine on parchment white,
'Midst war's resistless and ensanguined flood;
Then held that proclamation high in sight
Before his fratricidal countrymen,—
"Freedom henceforth throughout the land for all,"—
And sealed the instrument with his own blood,
Bowing his mighty strength for slavery's fall;
Whilst thou, stanch friend of largest liberty,
Survived,—its ruin and our peace to see.

RALPH WALDO EMERSON (1803–1882)

The poet, essayist, and lecturer was a leading exponent of New England Transcendentalism, an idealistic philosophical and social movement that was influenced by romanticism, Platonism, and Kantian philosophy. Transcendentalism promoted the belief that divinity pervades all nature and humanity, and that humans are innately good. Emerson's essays on nature and art had a tremendous impact on succeeding generations of American authors.

Boston *Sicut patribus, sit Deus nobis*

Read in Faneuil Hall, on December 16, 1873, on the Centennial Anniversary of the Destruction of the Tea in Boston Harbor.

> The rocky nook with hill-tops three
>   Looked eastward from the farms,
> And twice each day the flowing sea
>   Took Boston in its arms;
>   The men of yore were stout and poor,
>   And sailed for bread to every shore.
>
> And where they went on trade intent
>   They did what freeman can,
> Their dauntless ways did all men praise,
>   The merchant was a man.
>   The world was made for honest trade,—
>   To plant and eat be none afraid.
>
> The waves that rocked them on the deep
>   To them their secret told;
> Said the winds that sung the lads to sleep,
>   "Like us be free and bold!"
>   The honest waves refuse to slaves
>   The empire of the ocean caves.
>
> Old Europe groans with palaces,
>   Has lords enough and more;—
> We plant and build by foaming seas
>   A city of the poor;—
>   For day by day could Boston Bay
>   Their honest labor overpay.

We grant no dukedoms to the few,
　　We hold like rights and shall;—
Equal on Sunday in the pew,
　　On Monday in the mall.
　　　　For what avail the plough or sail,
　　　　Or land or life, if freedom fail?

The noble craftsman we promote,
　　Disown the knave and fool;
Each honest man shall have his vote,
　　Each child shall have his school.
　　　　A union then of honest men,
　　　　Or union nevermore again.

The wild rose and the barberry thorn
　　Hung out their summer pride
Where now on heated pavements worn
　　The feet of millions stride.

Fair rose the planted hills behind
　　The good town on the bay,
And where the western hills declined
　　The prairie stretched away.

What care though rival cities soar
　　Along the stormy coast:
Penn's town, New York, and Baltimore,
　　If Boston knew the most!

They laughed to know the world so wide;
　　The mountains said: 'Good-day!
We greet you well, you Saxon men,
　　Up with your towns and stay!'
　　　　The world was made for honest trade,—
　　　　To plant and eat be none afraid.

"For you," they said, "no barriers be,
　　For you no sluggard rest;
Each street leads downward to the sea,
　　Or landward to the West."

O happy town beside the sea,
   Whose roads lead everywhere to all;
Than thine no deeper moat can be,
   No stouter fence, no steeper wall!

Bad news from George on the English throne:
   "You are thriving well," said he;
"Now by these presents be it known,
   You shall pay us a tax on tea;
      'T is very small,—no load at all,—
      Honor enough that we send the call."

"Not so," said Boston, "good my lord,
   We pay your governors here
Abundant for their bed and board,
   Six thousand pounds a year.
(Your Highness knows our homely word,)
      Millions for self-government,
      But for tribute never a cent."

The cargo came! and who could blame
   If *Indians* seized the tea,
And, chest by chest, let down the same
   Into the laughing sea?
      For what avail the plough or sail,
      Or land or life, if freedom fail?

The townsmen braved the English king,
   Found friendship in the French,
And Honor joined the patriot ring
   Low on their wooden bench.

O bounteous seas that never fail!
   O day remembered yet!
O happy port that spied the sail
   Which wafted Lafayette!
      Pole-star of light in Europe's night,
      That never faltered from the right.

Kings shook with fear, old empires crave
   The secret force to find
Which fired the little State to save
   The rights of all mankind.

But right is might through all the world;
    Province to province faithful clung,
Through good and ill the war-bolt hurled,
    Till Freedom cheered and the joy-bells rung.

The sea returning day by day
    Restores the world-wide mart;
So let each dweller on the Bay
    Fold Boston in his heart,
        Till these echoes be choked with snows,
        Or over the town blue ocean flows.

Let the blood of her hundred thousands
    Throb in each manly vein;
And the wit of all her wisest,
    Make sunshine in her brain.
        For you can teach the lightning speech,
        And round the globe your voices reach.

And each shall care for other,
    And each to each shall bend,
To the poor a noble brother,
    To the good an equal friend.

A blessing through the ages thus
    Shield all thy roofs and towers!
God with the fathers, so with us,
    Thou darling town of ours!

Boston Hymn
Read in Music Hall, January 1, 1863.

The word of the Lord by night
To the watching Pilgrims came,
As they sat by the seaside,
And filled their hearts with flame.
God said, I am tired of kings,
I suffer them no more;
Up to my ear the morning brings
The outrage of the poor.
Think ye I made this ball

A field of havoc and war,
Where tyrants great and tyrants small
Might harry the weak and poor?
My angel,—his name is Freedom,—
Choose him to be your king;
He shall cut pathways east and west,
And fend you with his wing.
Lo! I uncover the land
Which I hid of old time in the West,
As the sculptor uncovers the statue
When he has wrought his best;
I show Columbia, of the rocks
Which dip their foot in the seas,
And soar to the air-borne flocks
Of clouds, and the boreal fleece.
I will divide my goods;
Call in the wretch and slave:
None shall rule but the humble,
And none but Toil shall have.
I will have never a noble,
No lineage counted great;
Fishers and choppers and ploughmen
Shall constitute a state.
Go, cut down trees in the forest,
And trim the straightest boughs;
Cut down trees in the forest,
And build me a wooden house.
Call the people together,
The young men and the sires,
The digger in the harvest field,
Hireling, and him that hires;
And here in a pine state-house
They shall choose men to rule
In every needful faculty,
In church, and state, and school.
Lo, now! if these poor men
Can govern the land and the sea,
And make just laws below the sun,
As planets faithful be.
And ye shall succor men;

'T is nobleness to serve;
Help them who cannot help again:
Beware from right to swerve.
I break your bonds and masterships,
And I unchain the slave:
Free be his heart and hand henceforth
As wind and wandering wave.
I cause from every creature
His proper good to flow:
As much as he is and doeth,
So much he shall bestow.
But, laying hands on another
To coin his labor and sweat,
He goes in pawn to his victim
For eternal years in debt.
To-day unbind the captive,
So only are ye unbound;
Lift up a people from the dust,
Trump of their rescue, sound!
Pay ransom to the owner,
And fill the bag to the brim.
Who is the owner? The slave is owner,
And ever was. Pay him.
O North! give him beauty for rags,
And honor, O South! for his shame;
Nevada! coin thy golden crags
With Freedom's image and name.
Up! and the dusky race
That sat in darkness long,—
Be swift their feet as antelopes,
And as behemoth strong.
Come, East and West and North,
By races, as snow-flakes,
And carry my purpose forth,
Which neither halts nor shakes.
My will fulfilled shall be,
For, in daylight or in dark,
My thunderbolt has eyes to see
His way home to the mark.

Concord Hymn
Sung at the completion of the
Concord Monument, April 19, 1836.

By the rude bridge that arched the flood,
    Their flag to April's breeze unfurled,
Here once the embattled farmers stood,
    And fired the shot heard round the world.

The foe long since in silence slept;
    Alike the Conqueror silent sleeps;
And Time the ruined bridge has swept
    Down the dark stream which seaward creeps.

On the green bank, by this soft stream,
    We set to-day a votive stone,
That memory may their deed redeem,
    When, like our sires, our sons are gone.

Spirit, that made those heroes dare
    To die, and leave their children free,
Bid Time and Nature gently spare
    The shaft we raise to them and Thee.

WILLIAM LLOYD GARRISON (1805–1879)

Garrison helped lead the successful abolitionist campaign against slavery in the United States through the pages of *The Liberator*, a newspaper he published from 1831 to 1865. Other causes he championed were temperance, women's rights, pacifism, and free trade.

Liberty for All

They tell me, Liberty! that in thy name
I may not plead for all the human race;
That some are born to bondage and disgrace,
Some to a heritage of woe and shame,
And some to power supreme, and glorious fame:

With my whole soul I spurn the doctrine base,
And, as an equal brotherhood, embrace
All people, and for all fair freedom claim!
Know this, O man! whate'er thy earthly fate—
God never made a tyrant nor a slave:
Woe, then, to those who dare to desecrate
His glorious image!—for to all He gave
Eternal rights, which none may violate;
And, by a mighty hand, the oppressed He yet shall save!

ROBERT MONTGOMERY BIRD
(1806–1854)

After one year of practicing medicine, Bird left to pursue a career as an author. He wrote poetry, novels, and plays—one of which, *The Gladiator,* had more than 1,000 performances in Bird's lifetime.

God Bless America!

Chorus:

> *God bless the land that gave us birth!*
>   *No pray'r but this know we.*
> *God bless the land, of all the earth,*
>   *The happy and the free.*
> *And where's the land like ours can brave*
>   *The splendor of the day,*
> *And find no son of hers a slave?*
>   *God bless America!*
> *God bless the land, the land beloved,*
>   *Forever and for aye!*
> *God bless the land that gave us birth.*
>   *God bless America!*

For liberty our grandsires trod
   The wide and stormy sea;
Our fathers bought it with their blood,
   Their children all are free;

And free, amid earth's servile hordes,
    To point the patriot's way,
With ploughshares turn'd in war to swords—
    God bless America.

Chorus

The desert howl'd—the pilgrim's came,
    They fled oppression's chain;
The desert blossom'd, and the flame
    Of freedom rose again.
And here, where hearts of fire are born,
    The flame shall ne'er decay,
While babes laugh kings and slaves to scorn—
    God bless America.

Chorus

And from our land, in hour of need,
    Avert Thy dark'ning frown;
Bind up all loyal hearts that bleed,
    And strike the traitor down.
And shall the serpent foe prevail?
    Shall friend, or fiend, betray?
Up with the star flag to the gale!
    God bless America.

Chorus

The banner of our Union loved
    Shall wave the ages on;
While time shall find no strife removed,
    No bright star quench'd and gone;
And kingly states, convulsed, shall die
    From earth be swept away;
Will millions will uphold the cry,
    God bless America.

Chorus

HENRY WADSWORTH LONGFELLOW
(1807–1882)

Easily remembered and recited poems such as "The Song of Hiawatha" and "Paul Revere's Ride" contributed to Longfellow's status as the most popular—although perhaps not the most talented or visionary—poet of the nineteenth century. The poet was also an educator and translator.

Excerpt from "The Building of the Ship"

Thou, too, sail on, O Ship of State!
Sail on, O UNION, strong and great!
Humanity with all its fears,
With all the hopes of future years,
Is hanging breathless on thy fate!
We know what Master laid thy keel,
What Workmen wrought thy ribs of steel,
Who made each mast, and sail, and rope,
What anvils rang, what hammers beat,
In what a forge and what a heat
Were shaped the anchors of thy hope!
Fear not each sudden sound and shock,
'T is of the wave and not the rock;
'T is but the flapping of the sail,
And not a rent made by the gale!
In spite of rock and tempest's roar,
In spite of false lights on the shore,
Sail on, nor fear to breast the sea
Our hearts, our hopes, are all with thee,
Our hearts, our hopes, our prayers, our tears,
Our faith triumphant o'er our fears,
Are all with thee,—are all with thee!

The Cumberland

At anchor in Hampton Roads we lay,
　　On board of the *Cumberland*, sloop-of-war;
And at times from the fortress across the bay
　　　The alarum of drums swept past,
　　　　Or a bugle blast
　　From the camp on the shore.

Then far away to the south uprose
    A little feather of snow-white smoke,
And we knew that the iron ship of our foes
      Was steadily steering its course
      To try the force
    Of our ribs of oak.

Down upon us heavily runs,
    Silent and sullen, the floating fort;
Then comes a puff of smoke from her guns,
      And leaps the terrible death,
      With fiery breath,
    From each open port.

We are not idle, but send her straight
    Defiance back in a full broadside!
As hail rebounds from a roof of slate,
      Rebounds our heavier hail
      From each iron scale
    Of the monster's hide.

"Strike your flag!" the rebel cries,
    In his arrogant old plantation strain.
"Never!" our gallant Morris replies;
      "It is better to sink than to yield!"
      And the whole air pealed
    With the cheers of our men.

Then, like a kraken huge and black,
    She crushed our ribs in her iron grasp!
Down went the *Cumberland* all a wrack,
      With a sudden shudder of death,
      And the cannon's breath
    For her dying gasp.

Next morn, as the sun rose over the bay,
    Still floated our flag at the mainmast head.
Lord, how beautiful was Thy day!
      Every waft of the air
      Was a whisper of prayer,
    Or a dirge for the dead.

> Ho! brave hearts that went down in the seas!
>   Ye are at peace in the troubled stream;
> Ho! brave land! with hearts like these,
>   Thy flag, that is rent in twain,
>   Shall be one again,
>   And without a seam!

Paul Revere's Ride

Listen, my children, and you shall hear
Of the midnight ride of Paul Revere.
On the eighteenth of April, in Seventy-Five;
Hardly a man is now alive
Who remembers that famous day and year.

He said to his friend,—"If the British march
By land or sea from the town to-night,
Hang a lantern aloft in the belfry-arch
Of the North-Church-tower as a signal-light,—
One if by land, and two if by sea;
And I on the opposite shore will be,
Ready to ride and spread the alarm
Through every Middlesex village and farm,
For the country-folk to be up and to arm."

Then he said good-night, and with muffled oar
Silently rowed to the Charlestown shore,
Just as the moon rose over the bay,
Where swinging wide at her moorings lay
The Somersett, British man-of-war;
A phantom ship, with each mast and spar
Across the moon, like a prison-bar,
And a huge, black hulk, that was magnified
By its own reflection in the tide.

Meanwhile, his friend, through alley and street
Wanders and watches with eager ears,
Till in the silence around him he hears
The muster of men at the barrack-door,
The sound of arms, and the tramp of feet,
And the measured tread of the grenadiers—
Marching down to their boats on the shore.

Then he climbed the tower of the church,
Up the wooden stairs, with stealthy tread,
To the belfry-chamber overhead,
And startled the pigeons from their perch
On the sombre rafters, that round him made
Masses and moving shapes of shade,—
Up the light ladder, slender and tall,
To the highest window in the wall,
Where he paused to listen and look down
A moment on the roofs of the town,
And the moonlight flowing over all.

Beneath, in the churchyard, lay the dead
In their night-encampment on the hill,
Wrapped in silence so deep and still,
That he could hear, like a sentinel's tread,
The watchful night-wind, as it went
Creeping along from tent to tent,
And seeming to whisper, "All is well!"
A moment only he feels the spell
Of the place and the hour, the secret dread
Of the lonely belfry and the dead;
For suddenly all his thoughts are bent
On a shadowy something far away,
Where the river widens to meet the bay,—
A line of black, that bends and floats
On the rising tide, like a bridge of boats.

Meanwhile, impatient to mount and ride,
Booted and spurred, with a heavy stride,
On the opposite shore walked Paul Revere.
Now he patted his horse's side,
Now gazed on the landscape far and near,
Then impetuous stamped the earth,
And turned and tightened his saddle-girth;
But mostly he watched with eager search
The belfry-tower of the Old North Church,
As it rose above the graves on the hill,
Lonely, and spectral, and sombre, and still.

And lo! as he looks, on the belfry's height,
A glimmer, and then a gleam of light!
He springs to the saddle, the bridle he turns,
But lingers and gazes, till full on his sight
A second lamp in the belfry burns!

A hurry of hoofs in a village-street,
A shape in the moonlight, a bulk in the dark,
And beneath from the pebbles, in passing, a spark
Struck out by a steed that flies fearless and fleet:
That was all! And yet, through the gloom and the light,
The fate of a nation was riding that night;
And the spark struck out by that steed, in his flight,
Kindled the land into flame with its heat.

He has left the village and mounted the steep,
And beneath him, tranquil and broad and deep,
Is the Mystic, meeting the ocean tides;
And under the alders that skirt its edge,
Now soft on the sand, now loud on the ledge,
Is heard the tramp of his steed as he rides.

It was twelve by the village-clock,
When he crossed the bridge into Medford town.
He heard the crowing of the cock,
And the barking of the farmer's dog,
And felt the damp of the river fog,
That rises when the sun goes down.

It was one by the village clock,
When he rode into Lexington.
He saw the gilded weathercock
Swim in the moonlight as he passed,
And the meeting-house windows, blank and bare,
Gaze at him with a spectral glare,
As if they already stood aghast
At the bloody work they would look upon.

It was two by the village-clock,
When he came to the bridge in Concord town.
He heard the bleating of the flock,
And the twitter of birds among the trees,
And felt the breath of the morning-breeze

Blowing over the meadows brown.
And one was safe and asleep in his bed
Who at the bridge would be first to fall,
Who that day would be lying dead,
Pierced by a British musket-ball.

You know the rest. In the books you have read
How the British Regulars fired and fled,—
How the farmers gave them ball for ball,
From behind each fence and farmyard-wall,
Chasing the red-coats down the lane,
Then crossing the fields to emerge again
Under the trees at the turn of the road,
And only pausing to fire and load.

So through the night rode Paul Revere;
And so through the night went his cry of alarm
To every Middlesex village and farm,—
A cry of defiance, and not of fear,—
A voice in the darkness, a knock at the door,
And a word that shall echo forevermore!
For, borne on the night-wind of the Past,
Through all our history, to the last,
In the hour of darkness and peril and need,
The people will waken and listen to hear
The hurrying hoof-beat of that steed,
And the midnight-message of Paul Revere.

JOHN GREENLEAF WHITTIER (1807–1892)

If Henry Wadsworth Longfellow was the most popular nineteenth-century poet, Whittier was a close second. Readers in both England and the United States embraced his moral, often sentimental, verse. He was a prominent abolitionist and supporter of humanitarian causes.

Barbara Frietchie

Up from the meadows rich with corn,
Clear in the cool September morn,

The clustered spires of Frederick stand
Green-walled by the hills of Maryland.

Round about them orchards sweep,
Apple and peach tree fruited deep,

Fair as the garden of the Lord
To the eyes of the famished rebel horde,

On that pleasant morn of the early fall
When Lee marched over the mountain wall,

Over the mountains winding down,
Horse and foot, into Frederick town.

Forty flags with their silver stars,
Forty flags with their crimson bars,

Flapped in the morning wind: the sun
Of noon looked down, and saw not one.

Up rose old Barbara Frietchie then,
Bowed with her fourscore years and ten;

Bravest of all in Frederick town,
She took up the flag the men hauled down;

In her attic window the staff she set,
To show that one heart was loyal yet.

Up the street came the rebel tread,
Stonewall Jackson riding ahead.

Under his slouched hat left and right
He glanced; the old flag met his sight.

"Halt!"—the dust-brown ranks stood fast.
"Fire!"—out blazed the rifle-blast.

It shivered the window, pane and sash;
It rent the banner with seam and gash.

Quick, as it fell, from the broken staff
Dame Barbara snatched the silken scarf.

She leaned far out on the window-sill,
And shook it forth with a royal will.

"Shoot, if you must, this old gray head,
But spare your country's flag," she said.

A shade of sadness, a blush of shame,
Over the face of the leader came;

The nobler nature within him stirred
To life at that woman's deed and word:

"Who touches a hair of yon gray head
Dies like a dog! March on!" he said.

All day long through Frederick street
Sounded the tread of marching feet:

All day long that free flag tost
Over the heads of the rebel host.

Ever its torn folds rose and fell
On the loyal winds that loved it well;

And through the hill-gaps sunset light
Shone over it with a warm good-night.

Barbara Frietchie's work is o'er,
And the Rebel rides on his raids no more.

Honor to her! and let a tear
Fall, for her sake, on Stonewall's bier.

Over Barbara Frietchie's grave,
Flag of Freedom and Union, wave!

Peace and order and beauty draw
Round thy symbol of light and law;

And ever the stars above look down
On thy stars below in Frederick town!

Centennial Hymn
Written for the opening of the international exhibition, Philadelphia, May 10, 1876.

I.

Our father's God! from out whose hand
The centuries fall like grains of sand,
We meet to-day, united, free,
And loyal to our land and Thee,
To thank Thee for the era done,
And trust Thee for the opening one.

II.

Here, where of old, by Thy design,
The fathers spake that word of Thine
Whose echo is the glad refrain
Of rended bolt and falling chain,
To grace our festal time, from all
The zones of earth our guests we call.

III.

Be with us while the New World greets
The Old World thronging all its streets,
Unveiling all the triumphs won
By art or toil beneath the sun;
And unto common good ordain
This rivalship of hand and brain.

IV.

Thou, who hast here in concord furled
The war flags of a gathered world,
Beneath our Western skies fulfill
The Orient's mission of good-will,
And, freighted with love's Golden Fleece,
Send back its Argonauts of peace.

V.

For art and labor met in truce,
And beauty made the bride of use,
We thank Thee; but, withal, we crave
The austere virtues strong to save,
The honor proof to place or gold,
The manhood never bought nor sold!

VI.

Oh make Thou us, through centuries long,
In peace secure, in justice strong;
Around our gift of freedom draw
The safeguards of Thy righteous law:
And, cast in some diviner mould,
Let the new cycle shame the old!

Our Country

WE give thy natal day to hope,
O Country of our love and prayer!
Thy way is down no fatal slope,
But up to freer sun and air.

Tried as by furnace-fires, and yet
By God's grace only stronger made,
In future tasks before thee set
Thou shalt not lack the old-time aid.

The fathers sleep, but men remain
As wise, as true, and brave as they;
Why count the loss and not the gain?
The best is that we have to-day.

Whate'er of folly, shame, or crime,
Within thy mighty bounds transpires,
With speed defying space and time
Comes to us on the accusing wires;

While of thy wealth of noble deeds,
Thy homes of peace, thy votes unsold,
The love that pleads for human needs,
The wrong redressed, but half is told!

We read each felon's chronicle,
His acts, his words, his gallows-mood;
We know the single sinner well
And not the nine and ninety good.

Yet if, on daily scandals fed,
We seem at times to doubt thy worth,
We know thee still, when all is said,
The best and dearest spot on earth.

From the warm Mexic Gulf, or where
Belted with flowers Los Angeles
Basks in the semi-tropic air,
To where Katahdin's cedar trees

Are dwarfed and bent by Northern winds,
Thy plenty's horn is yearly filled;
Alone, the rounding century finds
Thy liberal soil by free hands tilled.

A refuge for the wronged and poor,
Thy generous heart has borne the blame
That, with them, through thy open door,
The old world's evil outcasts came.

But, with thy just and equal rule,
And labor's need and breadth of lands,
Free press and rostrum, church and school,
Thy sure, if slow, transforming hands

Shall mould even them to thy design,
Making a blessing of the ban;
And Freedom's chemistry combine
The alien elements of man.

The power that broke their prison bar
And set the dusky millions free,
And welded in the flame of war
The Union fast to Liberty,

Shall it not deal with other ills,
Redress the red man's grievance, break
The Circean cup which shames and kills,
And Labor full requital make?

Alone to such as fitly bear
Thy civic honors bid them fall?
And call thy daughters forth to share
The rights and duties pledged to all?

Give every child his right of school,
Merge private greed in public good,
And spare a treasury overfull
The tax upon a poor man's food?

No lack was in thy primal stock,
No weakling founders builded here;
Thine were the men of Plymouth Rock,
The Huguenot and Cavalier;

And they whose firm endurance gained
The freedom of the souls of men,
Whose hands, unstained with blood, maintained
The swordless commonwealth of Penn.

And thine shall be the power of all
To do the work which duty bids,
And make the people's council hall
As lasting as the Pyramids!

Well have thy later years made good
Thy brave-said word a century back,
The pledge of human brotherhood,
The equal claim of white and black.

That word still echoes round the world,
And all who hear it turn to thee,
And read upon thy flag unfurled
The prophecies of destiny.

Thy great world-lesson all shall learn,
The nations in thy school shall sit,
Earth's farthest mountain-tops shall burn
With watch-fires from thy own uplit.

Great without seeking to be great
By fraud or conquest, rich in gold,
But richer in the large estate
Of virtue which thy children hold,

With peace that comes of purity
And strength to simple justice due,
So runs our loyal dream of thee;
God of our fathers! make it true.

O Land of lands! to thee we give
Our prayers, our hopes, our service free;
For thee thy sons shall nobly live,
And at thy need shall die for thee!

The Poor Voter on Election Day

The proudest now is but my peer,
    The highest not more high;
To-day, of all the weary year,
    A king of men am I.
To-day, alike are great and small,
    The nameless and the known;
My palace is the people's hall,
    The ballot-box my throne!

Who serves to-day upon the list
    Beside the served shall stand;
Alike the brown and wrinkled fist,
    The gloved and dainty hand!
The rich is level with the poor,
    The weak is strong to-day;
And sleekest broadcloth counts no more
    Than homespun frock of gray.

To-day let pomp and vain pretence
    My stubborn right abide;
I set a plain man's common sense
    Against the pedant's pride.
To-day shall simple manhood try
    The strength of gold and land;
The wide world has not wealth to buy
    The power in my right hand!

While there's a grief to seek redress
    Or balance to adjust,
Where weighs our living manhood less
    Than Mammon's vilest dust,—
While there's a right to need my vote,
    A wrong to sweep away,
Up! clouted knee and ragged coat!
    A man's a man to-day!

The Pumpkin

Oh, greenly and fair in the lands of the sun,
The vines of the gourd and the rich melon run,
And the rock and the tree and the cottage enfold,
With broad leaves all greenness and blossoms all gold,
Like that which o'er Nineveh's prophet once grew,
While he waited to know that his warning was true,
And longed for the storm-cloud, and listened in vain
For the rush of the whirlwind and red fire-rain.

On the banks of the Xenil the dark Spanish maiden
Comes up with the fruit of the tangled vine laden;
And the Creole of Cuba laughs out to behold
Through orange-leaves shining the broad spheres of gold;
Yet with dearer delight from his home in the North,
On the fields of his harvest the Yankee looks forth,
Where crook-necks are coiling and yellow fruit shines,
And the sun of September melts down on his vines.

Ah! on Thanksgiving day, when from East and from West,
From North and from South come the pilgrim and guest;
When the gray-haired New-Englander sees round his board
The old broken links of affection restored,
When the care-wearied man seeks his mother once more,
And the worn matron smiles where the girl smiled before,
What moistens the lip and what brightens the eye?
What calls back the past, like the rich Pumpkin pie?

Oh,—fruit loved of boyhood!—the old days recalling,
When wood-grapes were purpling and brown nuts were falling!
When wild, ugly faces we carved in its skin,
Glaring out through the dark with a candle within!

When we laughed round the corn-heap, with hearts all in tune,
Our chair a broad pumpkin,—our lantern the moon,
Telling tales of the fairy who travelled like steam,
In a pumpkin-shell coach, with two rats for her team!

Then thanks for thy present!—none sweeter or better
E'er smoked from an oven or circled a platter!
Fairer hands never wrought at a pastry more fine,
Brighter eyes never watched o'er its baking, than thine!
And the prayer, which my mouth is too full to express,
Swells my heart that thy shadow may never be less;
That the days of thy lot may be lengthened below,
And the fame of thy worth like a pumpkin-vine grow,
And thy life be as sweet, and its last sunset sky
Golden-tinted and fair as thy own Pumpkin pie!

SAMUEL FRANCIS SMITH (1808–1895)

Smith's song "America" was one of a handful of songs that was regarded as
the American national anthem before "The Star-Spangled Banner" received
official sanction from Congress in 1931. An author and Baptist minister, Smith
composed his song to the music of Great Britain's "God Save the King." This
is the original version; he added a stanza in 1889 for the Washington Centennial
Celebration.

America (or National Hymn)

My country, 't is of thee,
Sweet land of liberty,
    Of thee I sing;
Land where my fathers died,
Land of the pilgrims' pride,
From every mountain-side
    Let freedom ring.

My native country, thee
Land of the noble free,—
    Thy name I love;
I love thy rocks and rills,

Thy woods and templed hills;
My heart with rapture thrills
    Like that above.

Let music swell the breeze,
And ring from all the trees,
    Sweet freedom's song:
Let mortal tongues awake;
Let all that breathe partake;
Let rocks their silence break,—
    The sound prolong.

Our fathers' God, to thee,
Author of liberty,
    To thee I sing:
Long may our land be bright
With freedom's holy light;
Protect us by thy might,
    Great God, our King.

ALFRED, LORD TENNYSON (1809–1892)

Born in Lincolnshire, England, Tennyson was a popular poet during the reign of Queen Victoria and the first to be raised to the peerage for his writing. He was Poet Laureate of England for more than forty years.

England and America in 1782

O THOU, that sendest out the man
    To rule by land and sea,
Strong mother of a Lion-line,
Be proud of those strong sons of thine
    Who wrench'd their rights from thee!

What wonder, if in noble heat
    Those men thine arms withstood,
Retaught the lesson thou hadst taught,
And in thy spirit with thee fought,—
    Who sprang from English blood!

But Thou rejoice with liberal joy,
    Lift up thy rocky face,
And shatter, when the storms are black,
In many a streaming torrent back,
    The seas that shock thy base!

Whatever harmonies of law
    The growing world assume,
Thy work is thine—The single note
From that deep chord which Hampden smote
    Will vibrate to the doom.

OLIVER WENDELL HOLMES, SR.
(1809–1894)

With a career in medicine—as a physician, anatomy professor, and dean of Harvard Medical School—Holmes still found time to write poems, comic verse, and essays. His poem "Old Ironsides" roused enough public sentiment to quash the destruction of the U.S.S. *Constitution*, an American fighting ship from the War of 1812.

God Save the Flag!

Washed in the blood of the brave and the blooming,
    Snatched from the altars of insolent foes,
Burning with star-fires, but never consuming,
    Flash its broad ribbons of lily and rose.

Vainly the prophets of Baal would rend it,
    Vainly his worshippers pray for its fall;
Thousands have died for it, millions defend it,
    Emblem of justice and mercy to all:

Justice that reddens the sky with her terrors,
    Mercy that comes with her white-handed train,
Soothing all passions, redeeming all errors,
    Sheathing the sabre and breaking the chain.

Borne on the deluge of old usurpations,
  Drifted our Ark o'er the desolate seas,
Bearing the rainbow of hope to the nations,
  Torn from the storm-cloud and flung to the breeze!

God bless the Flag and its loyal defenders,
  While its broad folds o'er the battle-field wave,
Till the dim star-wreath rekindle its splendors,
  Washed from its stains in the blood of the brave!

Old Ironsides

Ay, tear her tattered ensign down!
  Long has it waved on high,
And many an eye has danced to see
  That banner in the sky;
Beneath it rung the battle shout,
  And burst the cannon's roar:—
The meteor of the ocean air
  Shall sweep the clouds no more!

Her deck, once red with heroes' blood,
  Where knelt the vanquished foe,
When winds were hurrying o'er the flood,
  And waves were white below,
No more shall feel the victor's tread,
  Or know the conquered knee;
The harpies of the shore shall pluck
  The eagle of the sea!

O, better that her shattered hulk
  Should sink beneath the wave;
Her thunders shook the mighty deep,
  And there should be her grave;
Nail to the mast her holy flag,
  Set every threadbare sail,
And give her to the god of storms,
  The lightning and the gale!

Union and Liberty

Flag of the heroes who left us their glory,
   Borne through their battle-fields' thunder and flame,
Blazoned in song and illumined in story,
   Wave o'er us all who inherit their fame!
     Up with our banner bright,
     Sprinkled with starry light,
   Spread its fair emblems from mountain to shore,
     While through the sounding sky
     Loud rings the Nation's cry,—
   UNION AND LIBERTY! ONE EVERMORE!

Light of our firmament, guide of our Nation,
   Pride of her children, and honored afar,
Let the wide beams of thy full constellation
   Scatter each cloud that would darken a star!
     Up with our banner bright, etc.

Empire unsceptred! what foe shall assail thee,
   Bearing the standard of Liberty's van?
Think not the God of thy fathers shall fail thee,
   Striving with men for the birthright of man!
     Up with our banner bright, etc.

Yet if, by madness and treachery blighted,
   Dawns the dark hour when the sword thou must draw,
Then with the arms of thy millions united,
   Smite the bold traitors to Freedom and law!
     Up with our banner bright, etc.

Lord of the Universe! shield us and guide us,
   Trusting thee always, through shadow and sun!
Thou hast united us, who shall divide us?
   Keep us, O keep us the MANY IN ONE!
     Up with our banner bright,
     Sprinkled with starry light,
   Spread its fair emblems from mountain to shore,
     While through the sounding sky
     Loud rings the Nation's cry,—
   UNION AND LIBERTY! ONE EVERMORE!

A Voice of the Loyal North

We sing "Our Country's" song to-night
　With saddened voice and eye;
Her banner droops in clouded light
　Beneath the wintry sky.
We'll pledge her once in golden wine
　Before her stars have set:
Though dim one reddening orb may shine,
　We have a Country yet.

'T were vain to sigh o'er errors past,
　The fault of sires or sons;
Our soldier heard the threatening blast,
　And spiked his useless guns;
He saw the star-wreathed ensign fall,
　By mad invaders torn;
But saw it from the bastioned wall
　That laughed their rage to scorn!

What though their angry cry is flung
　Across the howling wave,—
They smite the air with idle tongue
　The gathering storm who brave;
Enough of speech! the trumpet rings;
　Be silent, patient, calm,—
God help them if the tempest swings
　The pine against the palm!

Our toilsome years have made us tame;
　Our strength has slept unfelt;
The furnace-fire is slow to flame
　That bids our ploughshares melt;
'T is hard to lose the bread they win
　In spite of Nature's frowns,—
To drop the iron threads we spin
　That weave our web of towns,

To see the rusting turbines stand
　Before the emptied flumes,
To fold the arms that flood the land
　With rivers from their looms,—

But harder still for those who learn
    The truth forgot so long;
When once their slumbering passions burn,
    The peaceful are the strong!

The Lord have mercy on the weak,
    And calm their frenzied ire,
And save our brothers ere they shriek,
    "We played with Northern fire!"
The eagle hold his mountain height,—
    The tiger pace his den!
Give all their country, each his right!
    God keep us all!   Amen!

HENRY PETERSON (1818–1891)

Peterson worked as the assistant editor of the *Saturday Evening Post* in Philadelphia for more than twenty years. He published two volumes of poems as well as several plays.

Excerpt from "An Ode for Decoration Day"

O GALLANT brothers of the generous South,
    Foes for a day and brothers for all time!
I charge you by the memories of our youth,
    By Yorktown's field and Montezuma's clime,
Hold our dead sacred—let them quietly rest
In your unnumbered vales, where God thought best.
Your vines and flowers learned long since to forgive,
And o'er their graves a broidered mantle weave:
Be you as kind as they are, and the word
Shall reach the Northland with each summer bird,
And thoughts as sweet as summer shall awake
Responsive to your kindness, and shall make
Our peace the peace of brothers once again,
And banish utterly the days of pain.

And ye, O Northmen! be ye not outdone
    In generous thought and deed.
We all do need forgiveness, every one:
    And they that give shall find it in their need.

Spare of your flowers to deck the stranger's grave,
　　Who died for a lost cause:—
A soul more daring, resolute, and brave,
　　Ne'er won a world's applause.
A brave man's hatred pauses at the tomb.
For him some Southern home was robed in gloom,
Some wife or mother looked with longing eyes
Through the sad days and nights with tears and sighs,
Hope slowly hardening into gaunt Despair.
Then let your foeman's grave remembrance share:
Pity a higher charm to Valor lends,
And in the realms of Sorrow all are friends.

JAMES RUSSELL LOWELL (1819–1891)

Lowell was a poet, critic, essayist, editor, professor, and diplomat—the archetypal "man of letters"—whose work extolled heroism and idealism. He was one of the five Fireside Poets, a group of nineteenth-century writers from New England whose work began to rival the popularity of British poets.

Excerpt from "An Ode for the Fourth of July, 1876" (I.2.)

What shape by exile dreamed elates the mind
Like hers whose hand, a fortress of the poor,
No blood in lawful vengeance spilt bestains?
Who never turned a suppliant from her door?
Whose conquests are the gains of all mankind?
To-day her thanks shall fly on every wind,
Unstinted, unrebuked, from shore to shore,
One love, one hope, and not a doubt behind!
Cannon to cannon shall repeat her praise,
Banner to banner flap it forth in flame:
Her children shall rise up to bless her name,
And wish her harmless length of days,
The mighty mother of a mighty brood,
Blessed in all tongues and dear to every blood,
The beautiful, the strong, and, best of all, the good!

Excerpts from "Ode Recited at the Harvard Commemoration, July 21, 1865"

VIII

We sit here in the Promised Land
  That flows with Freedom's honey and milk;
  But 't was they won it, sword in hand,
Making the nettle danger soft for us as silk.
  We welcome back our bravest and our best;—
  Ah me! not all! some come not with the rest,
Who went forth brave and bright as any here!
I strive to mix some gladness with my strain,
    But the sad strings complain,
    And will not please the ear:
I sweep them for a paean, but they wane
    Again and yet again
Into a dirge, and die away, in pain.
In these brave ranks I only see the gaps,
Thinking of dear ones whom the dumb turf wraps,
Dark to the triumph which they died to gain:
  Fitlier may others greet the living,
  For me the past is unforgiving;
    I with uncovered head
    Salute the sacred dead,
Who went, and who return not.—Say not so!
'T is not the grapes of Canaan that repay,
But the high faith that failed not by the way;
Virtue treads paths that end not in the grave;
No bar of endless night exiles the brave;
    And to the saner mind
We rather seem the dead that stayed behind.
Blow, trumpets, all your exultations blow!
For never shall their aureoled presence lack:
I see them muster in a gleaming row,
With ever-youthful brows that nobler show;
We find in our dull road their shining track;
    In every nobler mood
We feel the orient of their spirit glow,
Part of our life's unalterable good,

Of all our saintlier aspiration;
          They come transfigured back,
     Secure from change in their high-hearted ways,
     Beautiful evermore, and with the rays
     Of morn on their white Shields of Expectation!

XI

     Not in anger, not in pride,
     Pure from passion's mixture rude
     Ever to base earth allied,
     But with far-heard gratitude,
     Still with heart and voice renewed,
To heroes living and dear martyrs dead,
The strain should close that consecrates our brave.
     Lift the heart and lift the head!
          Lofty be its mood and grave,
          Not without a martial ring,
          Not without a prouder tread
          And a peal of exultation:
          Little right has he to sing
          Through whose heart in such an hour
          Beats no march of conscious power,
          Sweeps no tumult of elation!
          'T is no Man we celebrate,
          By his country's victories great,
A hero half, and half the whim of Fate,
          But the pith and marrow of a Nation
          Drawing force from all her men,
          Highest, humblest, weakest, all,
          For her time of need, and then
          Pulsing it again through them,
Till the basest can no longer cower,
Feeling his soul spring up divinely tall,
Touched but in passing by her mantle-hem.
Come back, then, noble pride, for 't is her dower!
          How could poet ever tower,
          If his passions, hopes, and fears,
          If his triumphs and his tears,
          Kept not measure with his people?

Boom, cannon, boom to all the winds and waves!
Clash out, glad bells, from every rocking steeple!
Banners, a-dance with triumph, bend your staves!
   And from every mountain-peak
   Let beacon-fire to answering beacon speak,
   Katahdin tell Monadnock, Whiteface he,
And so leap on in light from sea to sea,
     Till the glad news be sent
     Across a kindling continent,
Making earth feel more firm and air breathe braver:
  "Be proud! for she is saved, and all have helped to save her!
She that lifts up the manhood of the poor,
She of the open soul and open door,
With room about her hearth for all mankind!
The fire is dreadful in her eyes no more;
From her bold front the helm she doth unbind,
Sends all her handmaid armies back to spin,
  And bids her navies, that so lately hurled
  Their crashing battle, hold their thunders in,
  Swimming like birds of calm along the unharmful shore.
  No challenge sends she to the elder world,
  That looked askance and hated; a light scorn
  Plays o'er her mouth, as round her mighty knees
  She calls her children back, and waits the morn
Of nobler day, enthroned between her subject seas."

Excerpt from "Under the Old Elm" (V.3.)

Soldier and statesmen, rarest unison;
High-poised example of great duties done
Simply as breathing, a world's honors worn
As life's indifferent gifts to all men born;
Dumb for himself, unless it were to God,
But for his barefoot soldiers eloquent,
Tramping the snow to coral where they trod,
Held by his awe in hollow-eyed content;
Modest, yet firm as Nature's self; unblamed
Save by the men his nobler temper shamed;
Never seduced through show of present good
By other than unsetting lights to steer

New-trimmed in Heaven, nor than his steadfast mood
More steadfast, far from rashness as from fear;
Rigid, but with himself first, grasping still
In swerveless poise the wave-beat helm of will:
Not honored then or now because he wooed
The popular voice, but that he still withstood;
Broad-minded, higher-souled, there is but one
Who was all this and ours, and all men's,—WASHINGTON.

JULIA WARD HOWE (1819–1910)

Howe wrote "Battle-Hymn of the Republic" in 1861 during a visit to an army camp near Washington, D.C. After the poem was published a year later by the *Atlantic Monthly*, it became the semiofficial song of the Union Army. After the Civil War, Howe was heavily involved in the women's suffrage and peace movements. She was the first woman to be elected to the American Academy of Arts and Letters.

Battle-Hymn of the Republic

Mine eyes have seen the glory of the coming of the Lord:
He is trampling out the vintage where the grapes of wrath are stored;
He hath loosed the fateful lightning of His terrible swift sword:
   His truth is marching on.

I have seen Him in the watch-fires of a hundred circling camps;
They have builded Him an altar in the evening dews and damps;
I have read his righteous sentence by the dim and flaring lamps.
   His day is marching on.

I have read a fiery gospel, writ in burnished rows of steel:
"As ye deal with my contemners, so with you my grace shall deal;
Let the Hero, born of woman, crush the serpent with His heel,
   Since God is marching on."

He has sounded forth the trumpet that shall never call retreat;
He is sifting out the hearts of men before His judgment-seat:
Oh! be swift, my soul, to answer Him, be jubilant, my feet!
   Our God is marching on.

In the beauty of the lilies Christ was born across the sea,
With a glory in His bosom that transfigures you and me:
As He died to make men holy, let us die to make men free,
    While God is marching on.

WALT WHITMAN (1819–1892)

In *Leaves of Grass*, the collection of poems that Whitman repeatedly revised
and expanded, the poet produced a new style of American verse and use of
persona that continues to influence American authors today. Born a New
Yorker, Whitman spent many years in Washington, D.C., where he found
employment and made hundreds of hospital visits to soldiers wounded in the
Civil War. He relocated to Camden, New Jersey, after he had a stroke at the
age of fifty-three, and lived there until his death almost twenty years later. His
house in Camden is now a museum.

America

    Centre of equal daughters, equal sons,
    All, all alike endear'd, grown, ungrown, young or old,
    Strong, ample, fair, enduring, capable, rich,
    Perennial with the Earth, with Freedom, Law and Love,
    A grand, sane, towering, seated Mother,
    Chair'd in the adamant of Time.

Election Day, November, 1884

If I should need to name, O Western World, your powerfulest scene
    and show,
'Twould not be you, Niagara—nor you, ye limitless prairies—nor your
    huge rifts of canyons, Colorado,
Nor you, Yosemite—nor Yellowstone, with all its spasmic geyser-loops
    ascending to the skies,
    appearing and disappearing,
Nor Oregon's white cones—nor Huron's belt of mighty lakes—nor
    Mississippi's stream:
—This seething hemisphere's humanity, as now, I'd name—*the still
    small voice* vibrating—
    America's choosing day,

(The heart of it not in the chosen—the act itself the main, the quadrennial
    choosing,)
The stretch of North and South arous'd—sea-board and inland—Texas
    to Maine—the Prairie States—Vermont, Virginia, California,
The final ballot-shower from East to West—the paradox and conflict,
The countless snow-flakes falling—(a swordless conflict,
Yet more than all Rome's wars of old, or modern Napoleon's:) the
    peaceful choice of all,
Or good or ill humanity—welcoming the darker odds, the dross:
—Foams and ferments the wine? it serves to purify—while the heart
    pants, life glows:
These stormy gusts and winds waft precious ships,
Swell'd Washington's, Jefferson's, Lincoln's sails.

For You O Democracy

Come, I will make the continent indissoluble,
I will make the most splendid race the sun ever shone upon,
I will make divine magnetic lands,
   With the love of comrades,
     With the life-long love of comrades.

I will plant companionship thick as trees along all the rivers of America,
    and along the shores of the great lakes, and all over the prairies,
I will make inseparable cities with their arms about each other's necks,
   By the love of comrades,
     By the manly love of comrades.

For you these from me, O Democracy, to serve you ma femme!
For you, for you I am trilling these songs.

I Hear America Singing

I hear America singing, the varied carols I hear,
Those of mechanics, each one singing his as it should be blithe and
    strong,
The carpenter singing his as he measures his plank or beam,
The mason singing his as he makes ready for work, or leaves off work,
The boatman singing what belongs to him in his boat, the deck-hand
    singing on the steamboat deck,

The shoemaker singing as he sits on his bench, the hatter singing as he
  stands,
The wood-cutter's song, the ploughboy's on his way in the morning,
  or at noon intermission or at sundown,
The delicious singing of the mother, or of the young wife at work, or
  of the girl sewing or washing,
Each singing what belongs to him or her and to none else,
The day what belongs to the day—at night the party of young fellows,
  robust, friendly,
Singing with open mouths their strong melodious songs.

Mannahatta

I WAS asking for something specific and perfect for my city,
Whereupon lo! upsprang the aboriginal name.

Now I see what there is in a name, a word, liquid, sane, unruly,
  musical, self-sufficient,
I see that the word of my city is that word from of old,
Because I see that word nested in nests of water-bays, superb,
Rich, hemm'd thick all around with sail ships and steam ships, an
  island sixteen miles long, solid-founded,
Numberless crowded streets, high growths of iron, slender, strong,
  light, splendidly uprising toward clear skies,
Tides swift and ample, well-loved by me, towards sundown,
The flowing sea-currents, the little islands, larger adjoining islands,
  the heights, the villas,
The countless masts, the white shore-steamers, the lighters, the
  ferry-boats, the black sea-steamers well-modelled,
The down-town streets, the jobbers' houses of business, the houses
  of business of the ship-merchants and money-brokers, the
  river-streets,
Immigrants arriving, fifteen or twenty thousand in a week,
The carts hauling goods, the manly race of drivers of horses, the
  brown-faced sailors,
The summer air, the bright sun shining, and the sailing clouds aloft,
The winter snows, the sleigh-bells, the broken ice in the river,
  passing along up or down with the flood-tide or ebb-tide,
The mechanics of the city, the masters, well-form'd, beautiful-
  faced, looking you straight in the eyes,

Trottoirs throng'd, vehicles, Broadway, the women, the shops and
    shows,
A million people—manners free and superb—open voices—
    hospitality—the most courageous and friendly young men,
City of hurried and sparkling waters! city of spires and masts!
City nested in bays! my city!

Excerpts from "When Lilacs Last in the Dooryard Bloom'd"

1

When lilacs last in the dooryard bloom'd,
And the great star early droop'd in the western sky in the night,
I mourn'd, and yet shall mourn with ever-returning spring.

Ever-returning spring, trinity sure to me you bring,
Lilac blooming perennial and drooping star in the west,
And thought of him I love.

2

O powerful western fallen star!
O shades of night—O moody, tearful night!
O great star disappear'd—O the black murk that hides the star!
O cruel hands that hold me powerless—O helpless soul of me!
O harsh surrounding cloud that will not free my soul.

3

In the dooryard fronting an old farm-house near the white-wash'd
    palings,
Stands the lilac-bush tall-growing with heart-shaped leaves of rich
    green,
With many a pointed blossom rising delicate, with the perfume strong
    I love,
With every leaf a miracle—and from this bush in the dooryard,
With delicate-color'd blossoms and heart-shaped leaves of rich green,
A sprig with its flower I break.

6

Coffin that passes through lanes and streets,
Through day and night with the great cloud darkening the land,
With the pomp of the inloop'd flags with the cities draped in black,
With the show of the States themselves as of crape-veil'd women
  standing,
With processions long and winding and the flambeaus of the night,
With the countless torches lit, with the silent sea of faces and the unbared
  heads,
With the waiting depot, the arriving coffin, and the sombre faces,
With dirges through the night, with the thousand voices rising strong
  and solemn,
With all the mournful voices of the dirges pour'd around the coffin,
The dim-lit churches and the shuddering organs—where amid these
  you journey,
With the tolling tolling bells' perpetual clang,
Here, coffin that slowly passes,
I give you my sprig of lilac.

7

(Nor for you, for one alone,
Blossoms and branches green to coffins all I bring,
For fresh as the morning, thus would I chant a song for you O sane
  and sacred Death.

All over bouquets of roses,
O death, I cover you over with roses and early lilies,
But mostly and now the lilac that blooms the first,
Copious I break, I break the sprigs from the bushes,
With loaded arms I come, pouring for you,
For you and the coffins all of you O death.)

15

To the tally of my soul,
Loud and strong kept up the gray-brown bird,
With pure deliberate notes spreading filling the night.

Loud in the pines and cedars dim,
Clear in the freshness moist and the swamp-perfume,
And I with my comrades there in the night.

While my sight that was bound in my eyes unclosed,
As to long panoramas of visions.

And I saw askant the armies,
I saw as in noiseless dreams hundreds of battle-flags,
Borne through the smoke of the battles and pierc'd with missiles I saw
    them,
And carried hither and yon through the smoke, and torn and bloody,
And at last but a few shreds left on the staffs, (and all in silence,)
And the staffs all splinter'd and broken.

I saw battle-corpses, myriads of them,
And the white skeletons of young men, I saw them,
I saw the debris and debris of all the slain soldiers of the war,
But I saw they were not as was thought,
They themselves were fully at rest, they suffer'd not,
The living remained and suffer'd, the mother suffer'd,
And the wife and the child and the musing comrade suffer'd,
And the armies that remain'd suffer'd.

16

Passing the visions, passing the night,
Passing, unloosing the hold of my comrades' hands,
Passing the song of the hermit bird and the tallying song of my soul,
Victorious song, death's outlet song, yet varying ever-altering song,
As low and wailing, yet clear the notes, rising and falling, flooding the
    night,
Sadly sinking and fainting, as warning and warning, and yet again
    bursting with joy,
Covering the earth and filling the spread of the heaven,
As that powerful psalm in the night I heard from recesses,
Passing, I leave thee lilac with heart-shaped leaves,
I leave thee there in the door-yard, blooming, returning with spring.

I cease from my song for thee,
From my gaze on thee in the west, fronting the west, communing with
     thee,
O comrade lustrous with silver face in the night.

Yet each to keep and all, retrievements out of the night,
The song, the wondrous chant of the gray-brown bird,
And the tallying chant, the echo arous'd in my soul,
With the lustrous and drooping star with the countenance full of woe,
With the holders holding my hand nearing the call of the bird,
Comrades mine and I in the midst, and their memory ever to keep,
     for the dead I loved so well,
For the sweetest, wisest soul of all my days and lands—and this for his
     dear sake,
Lilac and star and bird twined with the chant of my soul,
There in the fragrant pines and the cedars dusk and dim.

O Captain! My Captain!

O Captain! my Captain! our fearful trip is done,
The ship has weather'd every rack, the prize we sought is won,
The port is near, the bells I hear, the people all exulting,
While follow eyes the steady keel, the vessel grim and daring;
     But O heart! heart! heart!
          O the bleeding drops of red,
               Where on the deck my Captain lies,
                    Fallen cold and dead.

O Captain! my Captain! rise up and hear the bells;
Rise up—for you the flag is flung—for you the bugle trills,
For you bouquets and ribbon'd wreaths—for you the shores a-crowding,
For you they call, the swaying mass, their eager faces turning;
     Here Captain! dear father!
          This arm beneath your head!
               It is some dream that on the deck,
                    You've fallen cold and dead.

My Captain does not answer, his lips are pale and still,
My father does not feel my arm, he has no pulse nor will,
The ship is anchor'd safe and sound, its voyage closed and done,
From fearful trip the victor ship comes in with object won;

Exult O shores, and ring O bells!
   But I with mournful tread,
      Walk the deck my Captain lies,
         Fallen cold and dead.

HERMAN MELVILLE (1819–1891)

Melville turned to writing poetry after his fiction failed to bring him financial security or sustained acclaim. He fared even worse with his poems: his book *Battle-Pieces and Aspects of the War* received little attention when it was privately published in 1886. Melville's poems have since been praised; his novel *Moby-Dick* is considered a classic.

On the Men of Maine
killed in the Victory of Baton Rouge, Louisiana

Afar they fell. It was the zone
   Of fig and orange, cane and lime
(A land how all unlike their own,
With the cold pine-grove overgrown),
   But still their Country's clime.
And there in youth they died for her—
      The Volunteers,
For her went up their dying prayers:
   So vast the Nation, yet so strong the tie.
What doubt shall come, then, to deter
   The Republic's earnest faith and courage high.

Rebel Color-Bearers at Shiloh

The color-bearers facing death
White in the whirling sulphurous wreath,
   Stand boldly out before the line;
Right and left their glances go,
Proud of each other, glorying in their show;
Their battle-flags about them blow,
   And fold them as in flame divine;
Such living robes are only seen
Round martyrs burning on the green—
And martyrs for the Wrong have been.

Perish their Cause! but mark the men—
Mark the planted statues, then
Draw trigger on them if you can.

The leader of a patriot-band
Even so could view rebels who so could stand;
    And this when peril pressed him sore,
Left aidless in the shivered front of war—
    Skulkers behind, defiant foes before,
And fighting with a broken brand.
The challenge in that courage rare—
Courage defenseless, proudly bare—
Never could tempt him; he could dare
Strike up the leveled rifle there.

Sunday at Shiloh, and the day
When Stonewall charged—McClellan's crimson May,
And Chickamauga's wave of death,
And of the Wilderness the cypress wreath—
        All these have passed away.
The life in the veins of Treason lags,
Her daring color-bearers drop their flags,
    And yield.   *Now* shall we fire?
        Can poor spite be?
Shall nobleness in victory less aspire
Than in reverse? Spare Spleen her ire,
        And think how Grant met Lee.

Sheridan at Cedar Creek
(October, 1864.)

Shoe the steed with silver
    That bore him to the fray,
When he heard the guns at dawning,—
        Miles away;
When he heard them calling, calling—
        Mount! nor stay:
        Quick, or all is lost;
        They've surprised and stormed the post,
        They push your routed host—
    Gallop! retrieve the day.

House the horse in ermine—
    For the foam-flake blew
White through the red October;
    He thundered into view;
They cheered him in the looming,
    Horseman and horse they knew.
        The turn of the tide began,
        The rally of bugles ran,
        He swung his hat in the van;
    The electric hoof-spark flew.

Wreathe the steed and lead him—
    For the charge he led
Touched and turned the cypress
    Into amaranths for the head
Of Philip, king of riders,
    Who raised them from the dead.
        The camp (at dawning lost),
        By eve, recovered—forced,
        Rang with laughter of the host
    At belated Early fled.

Shroud the horse in sable—
    For the mounds they heap!
There is firing in the Valley,
    And yet no strife they keep;
It is the parting volley,
    It is the pathos deep.
        There is glory for the brave
        Who lead, and nobly save,
        But no knowledge in the grave
    Where the nameless followers sleep.

THEODORE O'HARA (1820–1867)

O'Hara served in the military from the period spanning the Mexican-American War, which inspired his poem "Bivouac of the Dead," to the Civil War, where he was a colonel in the Confederate Army. Lines from O'Hara's elegy can be found in national cemeteries throughout the United States—most notably at the McClellan Gate at Arlington. Because O'Hara fought for the Confederacy, he is often not given credit for the inscriptions in places where both Union and Confederate soldiers are buried.

The Bivouac of the Dead

The muffled drum's sad roll has beat
   The soldier's last tattoo;
No more on Life's parade shall meet
   That brave and fallen few.
On Fame's eternal camping-ground
   Their silent tents are spread,
And Glory guards, with solemn round,
   The bivouac of the dead.

No rumor of the foe's advance
   Now swells upon the wind,
No troubled thought at midnight haunts
   Of loved ones left behind;
No vision of the morrow's strife
   The warrior's dream alarms;
No braying horn nor screaming fife
   At dawn shall call to arms.

Their shivered swords are red with rust,
   Their pluméd heads are bowed,
Their haughty banner, trailed in dust,
   Is now their martial shroud.
And plenteous funeral tears have washed
   The red stains from each brow,
And the proud forms, by battle gashed,
   Are free from anguish now.

The neighing troop, the flashing blade,
   The bugle's stirring blast,
The charge, the dreadful cannonade,
   The din and shout, are past;

Nor war's wild note nor glory's peal
   Shall thrill with fierce delight
Those breasts that nevermore may feel
   The rapture of the fight.

Like the fierce northern hurricane
   That sweeps his great plateau,
Flushed with the triumph yet to gain,
   Came down the serried foe,
Who heard the thunder of the fray
   Break o'er the field beneath,
Knew well the watchword of that day
   Was "Victory or Death."

Long had the doubtful conflict raged
   O'er all that stricken plain,
For never fiercer fight had waged
   The vengeful blood of Spain;
And still the storm of battle blew,
   Still swelled the gory tide;
Not long, our stout old chieftain knew,
   Such odds his strength could bide.

'T was in that hour his stern command
   Called to a martyr's grave
The flower of his beloved land,
   The nation's flag to save.
By rivers of their father's gore
   His firstborn laurels grew,
And well he deemed the sons would pour
   Their lives for glory too.

Full many a norther's breath has swept
   O'er Angostura's plain—
And long the pitying sky has wept
   Above its mouldered slain.
The raven's scream, or eagle's flight,
   Or shepherd's pensive lay,
Alone awakes each sullen height
   That frowned o'er that dread fray.

Sons of the dark and bloody ground,
    Ye must not slumber there,
Where stranger steps and tongues resound
    Along the heedless air.
Your own proud land's heroic soil
    Shall be your fitter grave;
She claims from war his richest spoil—
    The ashes of her brave.

Thus 'neath their parent turf they rest,
    Far from the gory field,
Borne to a Spartan mother's breast
    On many a bloody shield.
The sunshine of their native sky
    Smiles sadly on them here,
And kindred eyes and hearts watch by
    The heroes' sepulchre.

Rest on, embalmed and sainted dead!
    Dear as the blood ye gave;
No impious footstep here shall tread
    The herbage of your grave;
Nor shall your glory be forgot
    While Fame her record keeps,
Or Honor points the hallowed spot
    Where Valor proudly sleeps.

Yon marble minstrel's voiceless stone
    In deathless song shall tell,
When many a vanished age hath flown,
    The story how ye fell;
Nor wreck, nor change, nor winter's blight,
    Nor Time's remorseless doom,
Shall dim one ray of glory's light
    That gilds your deathless tomb.

GEORGE FREDERICK ROOT (1820–1895)

Root composed secular, religious, and martial songs, the latter of which became popular during the Civil War. President Lincoln's second call for Union troops inspired Root to write "The Battle-Cry of Freedom."

The Battle-Cry of Freedom

YES, we'll rally round the flag, boys, we'll rally once again,
    Shouting the battle-cry of freedom,
We will rally from the hill-side, we'll gather from the plain,
    Shouting the battle-cry of freedom.

Chorus:
The Union forever, hurrah! boys, hurrah!
    Down with the traitor, up with the star,
While we rally round the flag, boys, rally once again,
    Shouting the battle-cry of freedom.

We are springing to the call of our brothers gone before,
    Shouting the battle-cry of freedom,
And we'll fill the vacant ranks with a million freemen more,
    Shouting the battle-cry of freedom.

We will welcome to our numbers the loyal, true, and brave,
    Shouting the battle-cry of freedom,
And altho' they may be poor, not a man shall be a slave,
    Shouting the battle-cry of freedom.

So we're springing to the call from the East and from the West,
    Shouting the battle-cry of freedom,
And we'll hurl the rebel crew from the land we love the best,
    Shouting the battle-cry of freedom.

FRANCIS MILES FINCH (1827–1907)

A judge and academic, Finch wrote "The Blue and the Gray" after learning that, on Decoration Day in 1866, the women of a Columbus, Mississippi, memorial association lay flowers not only on the graves of Confederate soldiers but also on those of the Union dead.

The Blue and the Gray

By the flow of the inland river,
  Whence the fleets of iron have fled,
Where the blades of the grave-grass quiver,
  Asleep are the ranks of the dead:
    Under the sod and the dew,
      Waiting the Judgment-Day:—
    Under the one, the Blue;
      Under the other, the Gray.

These in the robings of glory,
  Those in the gloom of defeat,
All with the battle-blood gory,
  In the dusk of eternity meet:
    Under the sod and the dew,
      Waiting the Judgment-Day:—
    Under the laurel, the Blue;
      Under the willow, the Gray.

From the silence of sorrowful hours,
  The desolate mourners go,
Lovingly laden with flowers,
  Alike for the friend and the foe:
    Under the sod and the dew,
      Waiting the Judgment-Day:—
    Under the roses, the Blue;
      Under the lilies, the Gray.

So with an equal splendor,
  The morning sun-rays fall,
With a touch impartially tender,
  On the blossoms blooming for all:

Under the sod and the dew,
   Waiting the Judgment-Day:
Broidered withe gold, the Blue:
   Mellowed with gold, the Gray.

So, when the summer calleth,
  On forest and field of grain,
With an equal murmur falleth
  The cooling drip of the rain:
    Under the sod and the dew,
      Waiting the Judgment-Day:
    Wet with the rain, the Blue;
     Wet with the rain, the Gray.

Sadly, but not with upbraiding,
  The generous deed was done.
In the storm of the years that are fading
  No braver battle was won:
    Under the sod and the dew,
      Waiting the Judgment-Day:
    Under the blossoms, the Blue;
     Under the garlands, the Gray.

No more shall the war-cry sever,
  Or the winding rivers be red:
They banish our anger forever
  When they laurel the graves of our dead!
    Under the sod and the dew,
      Waiting the Judgment-Day:
    Love and tears for the Blue;
     Tears and love for the Gray.

GUY HUMPHREY MCMASTER (1829–1887)

At age twenty, while attending Hamilton College in New York, McMaster wrote "Carmen bellicosum," popularly known as "The Old Continentals." He became a lawyer and was later elected judge and surrogate of Steuben County, New York. Except for the occasional article and brief periods working as an editor, McMaster concentrated on law.

The Old Continentals (Carmen bellicosum.)

In their ragged regimentals
Stood the old Continentals,
    Yielding not,
When the grenadiers were lunging,
And like hail fell the plunging
    Cannon-shot;
    When the files
    Of the Isles
From the smoky night-encampment, bore the banner of the rampant
    Unicorn;
And grummer, grummer, grummer, roll'd the roll of the drummer
    Through the morn!

Then with eyes to the front all,
And with guns horizontal,
    Stood our sires;
And the balls whistled deadly,
And in streams flashing redly
    Blazed the fires;
    As the roar
    On the shore
Swept the strong battle-breakers o'er the green-sodded acres
    Of the plain;
An louder, louder, louder, crack'd the black gunpowder,
    Cracking amain!

Now like smiths at their forges
Worked the red St. George's
    Cannoneers;
And the villainous saltpetre

Rung a fierce, discordant metre
  Round their ears.
  As the swift
  Storm-drift,
With hot sweeping anger, came the horse-guards' clangor
  On our flanks;
Then higher, higher, higher, burn'd the old-fashion'd fire
  Through the ranks!

Then the bare-headed Colonel
Gallop'd through the white infernal
  Powder-cloud;
And his broadsword was swinging,
And his brazen throat was ringing
  Trumpet-loud.
  Then the blue
  Bullets flew,
And the trooper-jackets redden at the touch of the leaden
  Rifle-breath;
And rounder, rounder, rounder, roar'd the iron six-pounder,
  Hurling death!

PATRICK SARSFIELD GILMORE
(1829–1892)

After immigrating from Ireland when he was nineteen, Gilmore became a leading American bandmaster and virtuoso cornetist. When the Civil War started, all members of his Boston Brigade Band (later, Gilmore's Band) enlisted in the Union Army. Gilmore reputedly composed "When Johnny Comes Marching Home" in 1863 under the pseudonym of Louis Lambert. The song was sung by both Union and Confederate soldiers.

When Johnny Comes Marching Home

When Johnny comes marching home again,
  Hurrah! hurrah!
We'll give him a hearty welcome then,
  Hurrah! hurrah!
The men will cheer, the boys will shout,
The ladies, they will all turn out,

And we'll all feel gay,
When Johnny comes marching home.
   The men will cheer, the boys will shout,
   The ladies, they will all turn out,
     And we'll all feel gay,
   When Johnny comes marching home.

The old church-bell will peal with joy,
   Hurrah! hurrah!
To welcome home our darling boy,
   Hurrah! hurrah!
The village lads and lasses say,
With roses they will strew the way;
   And we'll all feel gay,
When Johnny comes marching home.

Get ready for the jubilee,
   Hurrah! hurrah!
We'll give the hero three times three,
   Hurrah! hurrah!
The laurel-wreath is ready now
To place upon his loyal brow,
   And we'll all feel gay,
When Johnny comes marching home.

Let love and friendship on that day,
   Hurrah! hurrah!
Their choicest treasures then display,
   Hurrah! hurrah!
And let each one perform some part,
To fill with joy the warrior's heart;
   And we'll all feel gay,
When Johnny comes marching home.
   The men will cheer, the boys will shout,
   The ladies, they will all turn out,
     And we'll all feel gay,
   When Johnny comes marching home.

JOEL BENTON (1832–1911)

In addition to writing poetry, New York-based author Benton wrote a biography of showman and businessman Phineas Taylor (P.T.) Barnum as well as books about Ralph Waldo Emerson and Edgar Allan Poe.

Grover Cleveland

Bring cypress, rosemary and rue
For him who kept his rudder true;
Who held to right the people's will,
And for whose foes we love him still.

A man of Plutarch's marble mold,
Of virtues strong and manifold,
Who spurned the incense of the hour,
And made the nation's weal his dower.

His sturdy, rugged sense of right
Put selfish purpose out of sight;
Slowly he thought, but long and well,
With temper imperturbable.

Bring cypress, rosemary and rue
For him who kept his rudder true;
Who went at dawn to that high star
Where Washington and Lincoln are.

SARAH CHAUNCEY WOOLSEY (1835–1905)

Under the pen name Susan Coolidge, Woolsey wrote a series of popular children's books that were inspired by her youth in Connecticut; her depiction of high-spirited heroines was unusual for the era. She also published verse, magazine articles, and scholarly titles. During the Civil War, she assisted in hospital work.

The Better Way

WHO serves his country best?
Not he who, for a brief and stormy space,
Leads forth her armies to the fierce affray.
Short is the time of turmoil and unrest,
Long years of peace succeed it and replace:
    There is a better way.

Who serves his country best?
Not he who guides her senates in debate,
And makes the laws which are her prop and stay;
Not he who wears the poet's purple vest,
And sings her songs of love and grief and fate:
    There is a better way.

He serves his country best,
Who joins the tide that lifts her nobly on;
For speech has myriad tongues for every day,
And song but one; and law within the breast
Is stronger than the graven law on stone:
    There is a better way.

He serves his country best
Who lives pure life, and doeth righteous deed,
And walks straight paths, however others stray,
And leaves his sons as uttermost bequest
A stainless record which all men may read:
    This is the better way.

No drop but serves the slowly lifting tide,
No dew but has an errand to some flower,
No smallest star but sheds some helpful ray,
And man by man, each giving to all the rest,
Makes the firm bulwark of the country's power:
    There is no better way.

JOHN JAMES PIATT (1835–1917)

During the Civil War, Piatt worked in the Treasury Department in Washington, D.C. Later he became librarian of the House of Representatives, then United States consul at Cork, Ireland.

The Mower in Ohio

The bees in the clover are making honey, and I am making my hay;
The air is fresh, I seem to draw a young man's breath to-day.

The bees and I are alone in the grass: the air is so very still
I hear the dam, so loud, that shines beyond the sullen mill.

Yes, the air is so still that I hear almost the sounds I cannot hear—
That, when no other sound is plain, ring in my empty ear:

The chime of striking scythes, the fall of the heavy swaths they sweep—
They ring about me, resting, when I waver half asleep;

So still, I am not sure if a cloud, low down, unseen there be,
Or if something brings a rumor home of the cannon so far from me:

Far away in Virginia, where Joseph and Grant, I know,
Will tell them what I meant when first I had my mowers go!

Joseph, he is my eldest one, the only boy of my three
Whose shadow can darken my door again, and lighten my heart for
    me.

Joseph, he is my eldest—how his scythe was striking ahead!
William was better at shorter heats, but Jo in the long run led.

William, he was my youngest; John, between them I somehow see,
When my eyes are shut, with a little board at his head in Tennessee.

But William came home one morning early, from Gettysburg, last July,
(The mowing was over already; although the only mower was I):

William, my captain, came home for good to his mother; and I'll be
    bound
We were proud and cried to see the flag that wrapt his coffin around;

For a company from the town came up ten miles with music and gun:
It seemed his country claimed him then—as well as his mother—her
    son.

But Joseph is yonder with Grant to-day, a thousand miles or near,
And only the bees are broad at work with me in the clover here.

Was it a murmur of thunder I heard that hummed again in the air?
Yet, may be, the cannon are sounding now their Onward to Richmond
  there.

But under the beech by the orchard, at noon, I sat an hour it would
  seem—
It may be I slept a minute, too, or wavered into a dream.

For I saw my boys, across the field, by the flashes as they went,
Tramping a steady tramp as of old, with the strength in their arms
  unspent;

Tramping a steady tramp, they came with flashes of silver that shone,
Every step, from their scythes that rang as if they needed the stone—

(The field is wide, and heavy with grass)—and, coming toward me,
  they beamed
With a shine of light in their faces at once, and—surely I must have
  dreamed!

For I sat alone in the clover-field, the bees were working ahead.
There were three in my vision—remember, old man: and what if Joseph
  were dead!

But I hope that he and Grant (the flag above them both, to boot)
Will go into Richmond together, no matter which is ahead or afoot!

Meantime, alone at the mowing here—an old man somewhat gray—
I must stay at home as long as I can, making, myself, the hay.

And so another round—the quail in the orchard whistles blithe;—
But first I'll drink at the spring below, and whet again my scythe.

BRET HARTE (1836–1902)

From 1854 to 1871, Harte lived in California, where he became famous for his colorful writing about life in the West. He resigned a professorship at the University of California and moved East after the *Atlantic Monthly* agreed to pay him the highest rate of any American story-writer up to that time. His inability to sustain success, for personal and professional reasons, led him to Europe, where audiences continued to take pleasure in his larger-than-life tales of old California.

Caldwell of Springfield (New Jersey, 1780)

Here's the spot. Look around you. Above on the height
Lay the Hessians encamped. By that church on the right
Stood the gaunt Jersey farmers. And here ran a wall,—
You may dig anywhere and you'll turn up a ball.
Nothing more. Grasses spring, waters run, flowers blow,
Pretty much as they did ninety-three years ago.
Nothing more, did I say? Stay one moment; you've heard
Of Caldwell, the parson, who once preached the Word
Down at Springfield? What. No? Come—that's bad; why he had
All the Jerseys aflame. And they gave him the name
Of the "rebel high-priest." He stuck in their gorge,
For he loved the Lord God,—and he hated King George!
He had cause, you might say! When the Hessians that day
Marched up with Knyphausen they stopped on their way
At the "Farms," where his wife, with a child in her arms,
Sat alone in the house. How it happened none knew
But God—and that one of the hireling crew
Who fired the shot! Enough!—there she lay,
And Caldwell, the chaplain, her husband, away!
Did he preach—did he pray? Think of him as you stand
By the old church to-day;—think of him and his band
Of militant ploughboys! See the smoke and the heat
Of that reckless advance,—of that straggling retreat!
Keep the ghost of that wife, foully slain, in your view,—
And what could you, what should you, what would you do?
Why, just what he did! They were left in the lurch
For the want of more wadding. He ran to the church,
Broke the door, stripped the pews, and dashed out in the road
With his arms full of hymn-books, and threw down his load

At their feet! Then, above all the shouting and shots,
Rang his voice,—"Put Watts into 'em,—Boys, give 'em Watts!"
And they did. That is all. Grasses spring, flowers blow,
Pretty much as they did ninety-three years ago.
You may dig anywhere and you'll turn up a ball,—
But not always a hero like this,—and that's all.

California's Greetings to Seward 1869

We know him well: no need of praise
  Or bonfire from the windy hill
To light to softer paths and ways
  The world-worn man we honor still;

No need to quote those truths he spoke
  That burned through years of war and shame
While History carves with surer stroke
  Across our map his noon-day fame;

No need to bid him show the scars
  Of blows dealt by the Scaean gate,
Who lived to pass its shattered bars,
  And see the foe capitulate;

Who lived to turn his slower feet
  Toward the western setting sun,
To see his harvest all complete,
  His dream fulfilled, his duty done,—

The one flag streaming from the pole,
  The one faith borne from sea to sea,—
For such a triumph, and such goal,
  Poor must our human greetings be.

Ah! rather that the conscious land
  In simpler ways salute the Man,—
The tall pines bowing where they stand,
  The bared head of El Capitan,

The tumult of the waterfalls,
  Pohono's kerchief in the breeze,
The waving from the rocky walls,
  The stir and rustle of the trees;

Till lapped in sunset skies of hope,
　　In sunset lands by sunset seas.
The Young World's Premier treads the slope
　　Of sunset years in calm and peace.

The Reveille

Hark! I hear the tramp of thousands,
　　And of armèd men the hum;
Lo! a nation's hosts have gathered
　　Round the quick-alarming drum,—
　　　　Saying: "Come,
　　　　Freemen, come!
Ere your heritage be wasted," said the quick-alarming drum.

"Let me of my heart take counsel:
　　War is not of Life the sum;
Who shall stay and reap the harvest
　　When the autumn days shall come?"
　　　　But the drum
　　　　Echoed: "Come!
Death shall reap the braver harvest," said the solemn-sounding drum.

"But when won the coming battle,
　　What of profit springs therefrom?
What if conquest, subjugation,
　　Even greater ills become?"
　　　　But the drum
　　　　Answered: "Come!
You must do the sum to prove it," said the Yankee-answering drum.

"What if, 'mid the cannons' thunder,
　　Whistling shot and bursting bomb,
When my brothers fall around me,
　　Should my heart grow cold and numb?"
　　　　But the drum
　　　　Answered: "Come!
Better there in death united than in life a recreant,—Come!"

Thus they answered—hoping, fearing,
　　Some in faith and doubting some,
Till a trumpet-voice proclaiming,
　　Said: "My chosen people, come!"

Then the drum,
Lo! was dumb,
For the great heart of the nation, throbbing, answered,
      "Lord, we come!"

JOAQUIN MILLER (1837–1913)

A lawyer, judge, and newspaper owner, Miller drew upon his youthful adventures in California's mining camps to write energetic, often overblown, verse about life in the West. Born Cincinnatus Hiner Miller, he took the name "Joaquin" as a pseudonym after writing an article about Joaquin Murrieta, a legendary bandit from Mexico.

Crossing the Plains

WHAT great yoked brutes with briskets low,
With wrinkled necks like buffalo,
With round, brown, liquid, pleading eyes,
That turn'd so slow and sad to you,
That shone like love's eyes soft with tears,
That seem'd to plead, and make replies,
The while they bow'd their necks and drew
The creaking load; and look'd at you.
Their sable briskets swept the ground,
Their cloven feet kept solemn sound.

Two sullen bullocks led the line,
Their great eyes shining bright like wine;
Two sullen captive kings were they,
That had in time held herds at bay,
And even now they crush'd the sod
With stolid sense of majesty,
And stately stepp'd and stately trod,
As if 't were something still to be
Kings even in captivity.

Preamble to "Kit Carson's Ride"

Room! room to turn round in, to breathe and be free,
To grow to be giant, to sail as at sea
With the speed of the wind on a steed with his mane
To the wind, without pathway or route or a rein.
Room! room to be free where the white border'd sea
Blows a kiss to a brother as boundless as he;
Where the buffalo come like a cloud on the plain,
Pouring on like the tide of a storm driven main,
And the lodge of the hunter to friend or to foe
Offers rest; and unquestion'd you come or you go.
My plains of America! Seas of wild lands!
From a land in the seas in a raiment of foam,
That has reached to a stranger the welcome of home,
I turn to you, lean to you, lift you my hands.
      London, 1871.

The Men of Forty-Nine

Those brave old bricks of forty-nine!
What lives they lived! what deaths they died!
A thousand cañons, darkling wide
Below Sierra's slopes of pine,
Receive them now. And they who died
Along the far, dim, desert route—
Their ghosts are many. Let them keep
Their vast possessions. The Piute,
The tawny warrior, will dispute
No boundary with these. And I
Who saw them live, who felt them die,
Say, let their unplow'd ashes sleep,
Untouch'd by man, on plain or steep.

The bearded, sunbrown'd men who bore
The burden of that frightful year,
Who toil'd, but did not gather store,
They shall not be forgotten. Drear

And white, the plains of Shoshonee
Shall point us to the farther shore,
And long, white, shining lines of bones,
Make needless sign or white mile-stones.

The wild man's yell, the groaning wheel;
The train that moved like drifting barge;
The dust that rose up like a cloud—
Like smoke of distant battle! Loud
The great whips rang like shot, and steel
Of antique fashion, crude and large,
Flash'd back as in some battle charge.

They sought, yea, they did find their rest.
Along that long and lonesome way,
These brave men buffet'd the West
With lifted faces. Full were they
Of great endeavor. Brave and true
As stern Crusader clad in steel,
They died a-field as it was fit.
Made strong with hope, they dared to do
Achievement that a host to-day
Would stagger at, stand back and reel,
Defeated at the thought of it.

What brave endeavor to endure!
What patient hope, when hope was past!
What still surrender at the last,
A thousand leagues from hope! how pure
They lived, how proud they died!
How generous with life! The wide
And gloried age of chivalry
Hath not one page like this to me.

Let all these golden days go by,
In sunny summer weather. I
But think upon my buried brave,
And breathe beneath another sky.
Let Beauty glide in gilded car,
And find my sundown seas afar,
Forgetful that 'tis but one grave
From eastmost to the westmost wave.

Yea, I remember! The still tears
That o'er uncoffin'd faces fell!
The final, silent, sad farewell!
God! these are with me all the years!
They shall be with me ever. I
Shall not forget. I hold a trust.
They are part of my existence. When
Swift down the shining iron track
You sweep, and fields of corn flash back,
And herds of lowing steers move by,
And men laugh loud, in mute mistrust,
I turn to other days, to men
Who made a pathway with their dust.
Naples, 1874.

Yosemite

Sound! sound! sound!
O colossal walls and crown'd
In one eternal thunder!
Sound! sound! sound!
O ye oceans overhead,
While we walk, subdued in wonder,
In the ferns and grasses, under
And beside the swift Merced!

Fret! fret! fret!
Streaming, sounding banners, set
On the giant granite castles
In the clouds and in the snow!
But the foe he comes not yet,—
We are loyal, valiant vassals,
And we touch the trailing tassels
Of the banners far below.

Surge! surge! surge!
From the white Sierra's verge,
To the very valley blossom.
Surge! surge! surge!
Yet the song-bird builds a home,
And the mossy branches cross them,
And the tasselled tree-tops toss them
In the clouds of falling foam.

Sweep! sweep! sweep!
O ye heaven-born and deep,
In one dread, unbroken chorus!
We may wonder or may weep,—
We may wait on God before us;
We may shout or lift a hand,—
We may bow down and deplore us,
But may never understand.

Beat! beat! beat!
We advance, but would retreat
From this restless, broken breast
Of the earth in a convulsion.
We would rest, but dare not rest,
For the angel of expulsion
From this Paradise below
Waves us onward and . . . we go.

FREDERICK L. HOSMER (1840–1929)

Hosmer, a graduate of Harvard College and the Harvard Divinity School, was a Unitarian minister who led a series of congregations in Massachusetts, Ohio, Missouri, and California. He often revised his hymns after they were published. He was minister emeritus of the First Unitarian Church of Berkeley, California, from 1915 until his death in 1929.

O Beautiful, My Country

"O Beautiful, my Country!"
    Be thine a nobler care
Than all thy wealth of commerce,
    Thy harvests waving fair:
Be it thy pride to lift up
    The manhood of the poor;
Be thou to the oppress'd
    Fair Freedom's open door!

For thee our fathers suffered;
    For thee they toiled and prayed;
Upon thy holy altar
    Their willing lives they laid.

Thou has no common birthright,
   Grand memories on thee shine,
The blood of pilgrim nations
   Commingled flows in thine.

O Beautiful, our Country!
   Round thee in love we draw;
Thine is the grace of Freedom,
   The majesty of Law.
Be Righteousness thy sceptre,
   Justice thy diadem;
And on thy shining forehead
   Be Peace the crowning gem!

SIDNEY LANIER (1842–1881)

Lanier was first flutist in the Peabody Orchestra, Baltimore, and an author of poems and potboilers. The tuberculosis that Lanier contracted when he was imprisoned in Maryland while fighting for the Confederacy plagued him for the rest of his life.

Song of the Chattahoochee

Out of the hills of Habersham,
   Down the valleys of Hall,
I hurry amain to reach the plain,
Run the rapid and leap the fall,
Split at the rock and together again,
Accept my bed, or narrow or wide,
And flee from folly on every side
With a lover's pain to attain the plain
   Far from the hills of Habersham,
   Far from the valleys of Hall.

All down the hills of Habersham,
   All through the valleys of Hall,
The rushes cried *Abide, abide,*
The wilful waterweeds held me thrall,
The laving laurel turned my tide,
The ferns and the fondling grass said *Stay,*

The dewberry dipped for to work delay,
And the little reeds sighed *Abide, abide,*
  Here in the hills of Habersham,
  Here in the valleys of Hall.

  High o'er the hills of Habersham,
    Veiling the valleys of Hall,
The hickory told me manifold
Fair tales of shade, the poplar tall
Wrought me her shadowy self to hold,
The chestnut, the oak, the walnut, the pine,
Overleaning, with flickering meaning and sign,
Said, *Pass not, so cold, these manifold*
    Deep shades of the hills of Habersham,
    These glades in the valleys of Hall.

  And oft in the hills of Habersham,
    And oft in the valleys of Hall,
The white quartz shone, and the smooth brook-stone
Did bar me of passage with friendly brawl,
And many a luminous jewel lone
—Crystals clear or a-cloud with mist,
Ruby, garnet, and amethyst—
Made lures with the lights of streaming stone
    In the clefts of the hills of Habersham,
    In the beds of the valleys of Hall.

  But oh, not the hills of Habersham,
    And oh, not the valleys of Hall
Avail: I am fain for to water the plain.
Downward the voices of Duty call —
Downward, to toil and be mixed with the main,
The dry fields burn, and the mills are to turn,
And a myriad flowers mortally yearn,
And the lordly main from beyond the plain
    Calls o'er the hills of Habersham,
    Calls through the valleys of Hall.

RICHARD WATSON GILDER (1844–1909)

During the Civil War, Gilder served as a private in Landis's Philadelphia Battery when eastern Pennsylvania was being threatened by the Confederate Army. Unable to complete his law studies after his father's death, he became a newspaper reporter and magazine editor. Gilder's interest in public affairs led him to found numerous clubs and associations; he was one of the founders of the Society of American Architects, the International Copyright League, and the Association for the Blind.

The Burial of Sherman

GLORY and honor and fame and everlasting laudation
For our captains who loved not war, but fought for the life of the
    nation;
Who knew that, in all the land, one slave meant strife, not peace;
Who fought for freedom, not glory; made war that war might cease.

Glory and honor and fame; the beating of muffled drums;
The wailing funeral dirge, as the flag-wrapt coffin comes.
Fame and honor and glory, and joy for a noble soul;
For a full and splendid life, and laurelled rest at the goal.

Glory and honor and fame; the pomp that a soldier prizes;
The league-long waving line as the marching falls and rises;
Rumbling of caissons and guns; the clatter of horses' feet,
And a million awe-struck faces far down the waiting street.

But better than martial woe, and the pageant of civic sorrow;
Better than praise of to-day, or the statue we build to-morrow;
Better than honor and glory, and History's iron pen,
Was the thought of duty done and the love of his fellow-men.

EMMA LAZARUS (1849–1887)

A poet, philanthropist, and essayist, Lazarus worked on behalf of Jewish immigrants and causes. She wrote "The New Colossus" to support the building of a pedestal for the Statue of Liberty in New York Harbor. While the poem was written in 1883, it was not until 1903, at the behest of the poet's friends, that a plaque with the text was mounted inside the pedestal.

The New Colossus

Not like the brazen giant of Greek fame,
With conquering limbs astride from land to land;
Here at our sea-washed, sunset gates shall stand
A mighty woman with a torch, whose flame
Is the imprisoned lightning, and her name
Mother of Exiles. From her beacon-hand
Glows world-wide welcome; her mild eyes command
The air-bridged harbor that twin cities frame.
"Keep ancient lands, your storied pomp!" cries she
With silent lips. "Give me your tired, your poor,
Your huddled masses yearning to breathe free,
The wretched refuse of your teeming shore.
Send these, the homeless, tempest-tost to me,
I lift my lamp beside the golden door!"

JOHN PHILIP SOUSA (1854–1932)

After enlisting in the United States Marine Corps at age thirteen and apprenticing with the Marine Band, Sousa, the son of Portuguese and Bavarian immigrants, became a popular bandmaster and prolific composer of military marches and other music. He toured the United States and Europe with his band before embarking on a world tour in 1910.

The Stars and Stripes Forever

Let martial note in triumph float,
And liberty extend its mighty hand;
A flag appears 'mid thunderous cheers,
The banner of the Western-land.

The emblem of the brave and true,
Its folds protect no tyrant crew;
The red and white and starry blue
Is freedom's shield and hope.
Other nations may deem their flags the best
And cheer them with fervid elation,
But the flag of the North and South and West
Is the flag of flags, the flag of Freedom's nation.

Chorus:
Hurrah for the flag of the free!
May it wave as our standard forever
The gem of the land and the sea,
The banner of the right,
Let despots remember the day
When our fathers with mighty endeavor
Proclaimed as they marched to the fray,
That by their might and by their right,
It waves forever.

Let eagle shriek from lofty peak
The never ending watchword of our land;
Let summer breeze waft through the trees
The echo of the chorus grand.
Sing out for liberty and light,
Sing out for freedom and the right,
Sing out for Union and its might,
O patriotic sons.
Other nations may deem their flags the best
And cheer them with fervid elation,
But the flag of the North and South and West
Is the flag of flags, the flag of Freedom's nation.

MINNA IRVING (1856?–1940)

Minna Irving was one of several pen names of the poet, short story writer, and journalist Minna Odell. In 1899, Odell received a gold medal from the survivors of the U.S.S. *Maine* for her writings on the loss of the battleship in Havana Harbor, Cuba. In 1923, she was commissioned by the French government to write a poem for a tablet to be placed on the grave of Theodore Roosevelt's son Quentin, an aviator who died in France during WWI.

Betsy's Battle Flag

From dusk till dawn the livelong night
She kept the tallow dips alight,
And fast her nimble fingers flew
To sew the stars upon the blue.
With weary eyes and aching head
She stitched the stripes of white and red,
And when the day came up the stair
Complete across a carven chair
    Hung Betsy's battle flag.

Like shadows in the evening gray
The Continentals filed away,
With broken boots and ragged coats,
But hoarse defiance in their throats;
They bore the marks of want and cold,
And some were lame and some were old,
And some with wounds untended bled,
But floating bravely overhead
    Was Betsy's battle flag.

When fell the battle's leaden rain,
The soldier hushed his moans of pain
And raised his dying head to see
King George's troopers turn and flee.
Their charging column reeled and broke,
And vanished in the rolling smoke,
Before the glory of the stars,
The snowy stripes and scarlet bars
    Of Betsy's battle flag.

The simple stone of Betsy Ross
Is covered now with mold and moss,
But still her deathless banner flies,
And keeps the color of the skies.
A nation thrills, a nation bleeds,
A nation follows where it leads,
And every man is proud to yield
His life upon a crimson field
   For Betsy's battle flag!

ROBERT BRIDGES (1858–1941)

Not to be confused with the British poet of the same name, American author
Bridges was the Editor-in-Chief of *Scribner's Magazine* in New York City. He
was the good friend of two presidents: Woodrow Wilson and Theodore
Roosevelt.

A Toast to Our Native Land

Huge and alert, irascible yet strong,
We make our fitful way 'mid right and wrong.
One time we pour out millions to be free,
Then rashly sweep an empire from the sea!
One time we strike the shackles from the slaves,
And then, quiescent, we are ruled by knaves.
Often we rudely break restraining bars,
And confidently reach out toward the stars.

Yet under all there flows a hidden stream
Sprung from the Rock of Freedom, the great dream
Of Washington and Franklin, men of old
Who knew that freedom is not bought with gold.
This is the Land we love, our heritage,
Strange mixture of the gross and fine, yet sage
And full of promise—destined to be great.
Drink to our Native Land! God Bless the State!

At the Farragut Statue

To live a hero, then to stand
    In bronze serene above the city's throng;
Hero at sea, and now on land
    Revered by thousands as they rush along;

If these were all the gifts of fame—
    To be a shade amid alert reality,
And win a statue and a name—
    How cold and cheerless immortality!

But when the sun shines in the Square,
    And multitudes are swarming in the street,
Children are always gathered there,
    Laughing and playing round the hero's feet.

And in the crisis of the game—
    With boyish grit and ardor it is played—
You'll hear some youngster call his name:
    "The Admiral—he never was afraid!"

And so the hero daily lives,
    And boys grow braver as the Man they see!
The inspiration that he gives
    Still helps to make them loyal, strong, and free!

KATHARINE LEE BATES (1859–1929)

A graduate of Wellesley College, Bates taught English literature at her alma mater for forty years. In 1893, during a stay in Colorado, she took a trip to Pike's Peak, the nation's easternmost "fourteener"—a mountain that tops 14,000 feet above sea level. The magnificent view inspired her to write "America the Beautiful."

America the Beautiful

O beautiful for spacious skies,
    For amber waves of grain,
For purple mountain majesties
    Above the fruited plain!

America! America!
God shed His grace on thee
And crown they good with brotherhood
From sea to shining sea!

O beautiful for pilgrim feet,
Whose stern, impassioned stress
A thoroughfare for freedom beat
Across the wilderness!
America! America!
God mend thine every flaw,
Confirm thy soul in self-control,
Thy liberty in law!

O beautiful for heroes proved
In liberating strife,
Who more than self their country loved,
And mercy more than life!
America! America!
May God thy gold refine,
Till all success be nobleness,
And every grain divine!

O beautiful for patriot dream
That sees beyond the years
Thine alabaster cities gleam
Undimmed by human tears!
America! America!
God shed His grace on thee
And crown thy good with brotherhood
From sea to shining sea!

WILLIAM ORDWAY PARTRIDGE
(1861–1930)

A sculptor, Partridge received public commissions, primarily in New York City, to create statues of prominent historical figures such as Thomas Jefferson and Ulysses S. Grant. He wrote the poem "Nathan Hale" in part to help generate interest in his sculpture of the Revolutionary War patriot who was hanged by the British. The monument can be found in St. Paul, Minnesota.

Nathan Hale

One hero dies—a thousand new ones rise,
  As flowers are sown where perfect blossoms fall;
Then quite unknown, the name of Hale now cries
  Wherever duty sounds her silent call.

With head erect he moves and stately pace,
  To meet an awful doom—no ribald jest
Brings scorn or hate to that exalted face:
  His thoughts are far away, poised and at rest;

Now on the scaffold see him turn and bid
  Farewell to home, and all his heart holds dear.
Majestic presence!—all man's weakness hid,
  And all his strength in that last hour made clear:
"My sole regret, that it is mine to give
Only one life, that my dear land may live."

ELLA HIGGINSON (1861–1940)

Poet and fiction writer Higginson promoted arts, education, and women's rights in her hometown of Bellingham, Washington. She helped establish the city's first public library and served as campaign manager for Frances C. Axtell, the first woman elected to Washington's State House of Representatives.

Moonrise in the Rockies

The trembling train clings to the leaning wall
  Of solid stone; a thousand feet below
Sinks a black gulf; the sky hangs like a pall
  Upon the peaks of everlasting snow.

Then of a sudden springs a rim of light,
    Curved like a silver sickle. High and higher—
Till the full moon burns on the breast of night,
    And a million firs stand tipped with lucent fire.

The Statue

THAT I might chisel a statue, line on line,
    Out of a marble's chaste severities!
    Angular, harsh; no softened curves to please;
Set tears within the eyes to make them shine,
And furrows on the brow, deep, stern, yet fine;
    Gaunt, awkward, tall; no courtier of ease;
    The trousers bulging at the bony knees;
Long nose, large mouth . . . But ah, the light divine
Of Truth,—the light that set a people free!—
    Burning upon it in a steady flame,
    As sunset fires a white peak on the sky . . .
Ah, God! To leave it nameless and yet see
    Men looking weep and bow themselves and cry—
    "Enough, enough! We know thy statue's name!"

EDITH WHARTON (1862–1937)

Best known for her fiction about upper-class American society, Wharton also wrote poems and articles about the First World War. Due to her social connections, she was able to travel to the front lines in France and document her experiences for *Scribner's Magazine*. Her articles were collected in the book *Fighting France: From Dunkerque to Belport.*

You and You
To the American Private in the Great War

Every one of you won the war—
You and you and you—
Each one knowing what it was for,
And what was his job to do.

Every one of you won the war,
Obedient, unwearied, unknown,
Dung in the trenches, drift on the shore,
Dust to the world's end blow;
Every one of you, steady and true,
You and you and you—
Down in the pit or up in the blue,
Whether you crawled or sailed or flew,
Whether your closest comrade knew
Or you bore the brunt alone—

All of you, all of you, name after name,
Jones and Robinson, Smith and Brown,
You from the piping prairie town,
You from the Fundy fogs that came,
You from the city's roaring blocks,
You from the bleak New England rocks
With the shingled roof in the apple boughs,
You from the brown adobe house—
You from the Rockies, you from the Coast,
You from the burning frontier-post
And you from the Klondyke's frozen flanks,
You from the cedar-swamps, you from the pine,
You from the cotton and you from the vine,
You from the rice and the sugar-brakes,
You from the Rivers and you from the Lakes,
You from the Creeks and you from the Licks
And you from the brown bayou—
You and you and you—
You from the pulpit, you from the mine,
You from the factories, you from the banks,
Closer and closer, ranks on ranks,
Airplanes and cannons, and rifles and tanks,
Smith and Robinson, Brown and Jones,
Ruddy faces or bleaching bones,
After the turmoil and blood and pain
Swinging home to the folks again
Or sleeping alone in the fine French rain—
Every one of you won the war.

Every one of you won the war—
You and you and you—
Pressing and pouring forth, more and more,
Toiling and straining from shore to shore
To reach the flaming edge of the dark
Where man in his millions went up like a spark,
You, in your thousands and millions coming,
All the sea ploughed with you, all the air humming,
All the land loud with you,
All our hearts proud with you,
All our souls bowed with the awe of your coming!

Where's the Arch high enough,
Lads, to receive you,
Where's the eye dry enough,
Dears, to perceive you,
When at last and at last in your glory you come,
Tramping home?

Every one of you won the war,
You and you and you—
You that carry an unscathed head,
You that halt with a broken tread,
And oh, most of all, you Dead, you Dead!

Lift up the Gates for these that are last,
That are last in the great Procession.
Let the living pour in, take possession,
Flood back to the city, the ranch, the farm,
The church and the college and mill,
Back to the office, the store, the exchange,
Back to the wife with the babe on her arm,
Back to the mother that waits on the sill,
And the supper that's hot on the range.

And now, when the last of them all are by,
Be the Gates lifted up on high
To let those Others in,
Those Others, their brothers, that softly tread,
That come so thick, yet take no ground,
That are so many, yet make no sound,
Our Dead, our Dead, our Dead!

O silent and secretly-moving throng,
In your fifty thousand strong,
Coming at dusk when the wreaths have dropt,
And streets are empty, and music stopt,
Silently coming to hearts that wait
Dumb in the door and dumb at the gate,
And hear your step and fly to your call—
Every one of you won the war,
But you, you Dead, most of all!

JOSEPH B. STRAUSS (1870–1938)

Strauss was a civil engineer who, along with Charles Alton Ellis, was responsible for building the Golden Gate Bridge in San Francisco, California.

California

California, land of wonders;
Land where the Pacific thunders,
Where white Shasta seeks the skies,
Home of mighty Thamalpais;
Land of fabled treasure-trove,
Fragrant sunkist orange grove;
Giant sequoias' lifted heads,
Miles of golden poppy-beds;
Land of the Yosemite,
Cuirassed palm and olive tree;
Land where summer zephyrs blow,
'Neath the winter peaks of snow;
Land of orange-blossom scent,
Garden of the Continent;
There, where the Pacific thunders,
California, land of wonders.

JAMES WELDON JOHNSON (1871–1938)

Johnson was an educator, attorney, diplomat, editor, author, and champion of African American culture and causes. His multi-faceted career included collaborating with his brother, composer John Rosamond Johnson, on hundreds of songs. Their collaboration "Lift Every Voice and Sing" became an anthem for many African Americans. Johnson was a leader in the National Association for the Advancement of Colored People (NAACP).

Fifty Years (1863–1913)
On the Fiftieth Anniversary of the Signing of the Emancipation Proclamation

O brothers mine, to-day we stand
    Where half a century sweeps our ken,
Since God, through Lincoln's ready hand,
    Struck off our bonds and made us men.

Just fifty years—a winter's day—
    As runs the history of a race;
Yet, as we look back o'er the way,
    How distant seems our starting place!

Look farther back! Three centuries!
    To where a naked, shivering score,
Snatched from their haunts across the seas,
    Stood, wild-eyed, on Virginia's shore.

This land is ours by right of birth;
    This land is ours by right of toil;
We helped to turn its virgin earth,
    Our sweat is in its fruitful soil.

Where once the tangled forest stood,—
    Where flourished once rank weed and thorn,—
Behold the path-traced, peaceful wood,
    The cotton white, the yellow corn.

To gain these fruits that have been earned,
    To hold these fields that have been won,
Our arms have strained, our backs have burned,
    Bent bare beneath a ruthless sun.

That Banner which is now the type
    Of victory on field and flood—
Remember. its first crimson stripe
    Was dyed by Attucks' willing blood.

And never yet has come the cry—
    When that fair flag has been assailed—
For men to do, for men to die,
    That we have faltered or have failed.

We've helped to bear it, rent and torn,
    Through many a hot-breath'd battle breeze
Held in our hands, it has been borne
    And planted far across the seas.

And never yet,—O haughty Land,
    Let us, at least, for this be praised—
Has one black, treason-guided hand
    Ever against that flag been raised.

Then should we speak but servile words,
    Or shall we hang our heads in shame?
Stand back of new-come foreign hordes,
    And fear our heritage to claim?

No! stand erect and without fear,
    And for our foes let this suffice—
We've bought a rightful sonship here,
    And we have more than paid the price.

And yet, my brothers, well I know
    The tethered feet, the pinioned wings,
The spirit bowed beneath the blow,
    The heart grown faint from wounds and stings;

The staggering force of brutish might,
    That strikes and leaves us stunned and dazed;
The long, vain waiting through the night
    To hear some voice for justice raised.

Full well I know the hour when hope
    Sinks dead, and 'round us everywhere
Hangs stifling darkness, and we grope
    With hands uplifted in despair.

Courage! Look out, beyond, and see
    The far horizon's beckoning span!
Faith in your God-known destiny!
    We are part of some great plan.

Because the tongues of Garrison
    And Phillips now are cold in death,
Think you their work can be undone?
    Or quenched the fires lit by their breath?

Think you that John Brown's spirit stops?
    That Lovejoy was but idly slain?
Or do you think those precious drops
    From Lincoln's heart were shed in vain?

That for which millions prayed and sighed,
    That for which tens of thousands fought,
For which so many freely died,
    God cannot let it come to naught.

Lift Every Voice and Sing

1

Lift ev'ry voice and sing
Till earth and heaven ring,
    Ring with the harmonies of Liberty;
Let our rejoicing rise
High as the list'ning skies,
Let it resound loud as the rolling seas;
Sing a song full of the faith that the dark past has taught us,
Sing a song full of hope that the present has brought us;
Facing the rising sun
Of our new day begun,
Let us march on till victory is won.

2

Stony the road we trod,
Bitter the chast'ning rod
Felt in the days when hope had died;
Yet, with a steady beat,

Have not our weary feet
  Come to the place for which our fathers sighed,
We have come over a way that with tears has been watered,
We have come, treading our path thro' the blood of the slaughtered,
Out from the gloomy past,
Till now we stand at last
Where the white gleam of our bright star is cast.

3

God of our weary years,
God of our silent tears,
  Thou who hast brought us thus far on the way;
Thou who hast by Thy might,
Led us into the light,
Keep us forever in the path, we pray,
Lest our feet stray from the places, our God, where we met Thee,
Lest, our hearts drunk with the wine of the world, we forget Thee,
Shadowed beneath Thy hand,
May we forever stand,
True to our God, true to our Native Land.

PAUL LAURENCE DUNBAR (1872–1906)

Dunbar wrote novels, short stories, plays, and essays—in addition to poems—
about the black experience in late nineteenth-century America. Admirers and
supporters included Orville and Wilbur Wright, the aviators, and Dunbar's
high-school classmates in Dayton, Ohio; English composer Samuel Coleridge-
Taylor, with whom Dunbar collaborated on an operetta; James Weldon
Johnson; and President Theodore Roosevelt.

Ode for Memorial Day

Done are the toils and the wearisome marches,
  Done is the summons of bugle and drum.
Softly and sweetly the sky overarches,
  Shelt'ring a land where Rebellion is dumb.
Dark were the days of the country's derangement,
  Sad were the hours when the conflict was on,

But through the gloom of fraternal estrangement
   God sent his light, and we welcome the dawn.
O'er the expanse of our mighty dominions,
   Sweeping away to the uttermost parts,
Peace, the wide-flying, on untiring pinions,
   Bringeth her message of joy to our hearts.

Ah, but this joy which our minds cannot measure,
   What did it cost for our fathers to gain!
Bought at the price of the heart's dearest treasure,
   Born out of travail and sorrow and pain;
Born in the battle where fleet Death was flying,
   Slaying with sabre-stroke bloody and fell;
Born where the heroes and martyrs were dying,
   Torn by the fury of bullet and shell.
Ah, but the day is past: silent the rattle,
   And the confusion that followed the fight.
Peace to the heroes who died in the battle,
   Martyrs to truth and the crowning of Right!

Out of the blood of a conflict fraternal,
   Out of the dust and the dimness of death,
Burst into blossoms of glory eternal
   Flowers that sweeten the world with their breath.
Flowers of charity, peace, and devotion
   Bloom in the hearts that are empty of strife;
Love that is boundless and broad as the ocean
   Leaps into beauty and fullness of life.
So, with the singing of paeans and chorals,
   And with the flag flashing high in the sun,
Place on the graves of our heroes the laurels
   Which their unfaltering valor has won!

Lincoln

Hurt was the nation with a mighty wound,
And all her ways were filled with clam'rous sound.
Wailed loud the South with unremitting grief,
And wept the North that could not find relief.
Then madness joined its harshest tone to strife:
A minor note swelled in the song of life.

Till, stirring with love that filled his breast,
But still, unflinching at the right's behest,
Grave Lincoln came, strong-handed, from afar,
The mighty Homer of the lyre of war.
'Twas he who bade the raging tempest cease,
Wrenched from his harp the harmony of peace,
Muted the strings that made the discord,—Wrong,
And gave his spirit up in thund'rous song.
Oh, mighty Master of the mighty lyre,
Earth heard and trembled at thy strains of fire:
Earth learned of thee what Heav'n already knew,
And wrote thee down among her treasured few.

Frederick Douglass

A hush is over all the teeming lists,
    And there is pause, a breath-space in the strife;
A spirit brave has passed beyond the mists
    And vapors that obscure the sun of life.
And Ethiopia, with bosom torn,
Laments the passing of her noblest born.

She weeps for him a mother's burning tears—
    She loved him with a mother's deepest love.
He was her champion thro' direful years,
    And held her weal all other ends above.
When Bondage held her bleeding in the dust,
He raised her up and whispered, "Hope and Trust."

For her his voice, a fearless clarion, rung
    That broke in warning on the ears of men;
For her the strong bow of his pow'r he strung,
    And sent his arrows to the very den
Where grim Oppression held his bloody place
And gloated o'er the mis'ries of a race.

And he was no soft-tongued apologist;
    He spoke straightforward, fearlessly uncowed;
The sunlight of his truth dispelled the mist,
    And set in bold relief each dark-hued cloud;
To sin and crime he gave their proper hue,
And hurled at evil what was evil's due.

Through good and ill report he cleaved his way
    Right onward, with his face set toward the heights,
Nor feared to face the foeman's dread array,—
    The lash of scorn, the sting of petty spites.
He dared the lightning in the lightning's track,
And answered thunder with his thunder back.

When men maligned him, and their torrent wrath
    In furious imprecations o'er him broke,
He kept his counsel as he kept his path;
    'Twas for his race, not for himself, he spoke.
He knew the import of his Master's call,
And felt himself too mighty to be small.

No miser in the good he held was he,—
    His kindness followed his horizon's rim.
His heart, his talents, and his hands were free
    To all who truly needed aught of him.
Where poverty and ignorance were rife,
He gave his bounty as he gave his life.

The place and cause that first aroused his might
    Still proved its power until his latest day.
In Freedom's lists and for the aid of Right
    Still in the foremost rank he waged the fray;
Wrong lived; his occupation was not gone.
He died in action with his armor on!

We weep for him, but we have touched his hand,
    And felt the magic of his presence nigh,
The current that he sent throughout the land,
    The kindling spirit of his battle-cry.
O'er all that holds us we shall triumph yet,
And place our banner where his hopes were set!

Oh, Douglass, thou hast passed beyond the shore,
    But still thy voice is ringing o'er the gale!
Thou'st taught thy race how high her hopes may soar,
    And bade her seek the heights, nor faint, nor fail.
She will not fail, she heeds thy stirring cry,
She knows thy guardian spirit will be nigh,
And, rising from beneath the chast'ning rod,
She stretches out her bleeding hands to God!

JOSHUA HENRY JONES, JR. (1876?–1955)

Jones was a journalist, poet, and novelist who wrote the words for Boston's official song, "Dear Old Boston," and who once served as Boston's poet laureate. *By Sanction of Law,* his book about an interracial romance published in 1924, was based loosely on his life.

The Heart of the World

In the heart of the world is the call for peace—
    Up-surging, symphonic roar.
'Tis ill of all clashings; it seeks release
    From fetters of greed and gore.
The winds of the battlefields echo the sigh
    Of heroes slumbering deep,
Who gave all they had and now dreamlessly lie
    Where the bayonets sent them to sleep.
    Peace for the wealthy; peace for the poor;
    Peace on the hillside, and peace on the moor.

In the heart of the world is the call for love:
    For fingers to bind up the wound,
Slashed deep by the ruthless, harsh hand of might,
    When Justice is crushed to the ground.
'Tis ill of the fevers of fear of the strong—
    Of jealousies—prejudice—pride.
"Is there no ideal that's proof against wrong?"
    Man asks of the man at his side.
    Right for the lowly; right for the great;
    Right all to pilot to happiness' gate.

In the heart of the world is the call for love:
    White heart—Red—Yellow—and Black.
Each face turns to Bethlehem's bright star above,
    Though wolves of self howl at each back.
The whole earth is lifting its voice in a prayer
    That nations may learn to endure,
Without killing and maiming, but doing what's fair
    With a soul that is noble and pure.
    Love in weak peoples; love in the strong;
    Love that will banish all hatred and wrong.

In the heart of the world is the call of God;
    East—West—and North—and South.
Stirring, deep-yearning, breast-heaving call for God
    A-tremble behind each mouth.
The heart's ill of torments that rend men's souls.
    Skyward lift all faiths and hopes;
Across all the oceans the evidence rolls,
    Refreshing all life's arid slopes.
    God in the highborn; God in the low;
    God calls us, world-brothers. Hark ye! and know.

CARL SANDBURG (1878–1967)

Sandburg received two Pulitzer Prizes for his poetry and one in the history category for his biography of Abraham Lincoln. His Midwestern subject matter and free verse, heavily influenced by Whitman, made him one of the twentieth century's most popular poets.

Chicago

Hog Butcher for the World,
Tool Maker, Stacker of Wheat,
Player with Railroads and the Nation's Freight Handler;
Stormy, husky, brawling,
City of the Big Shoulders:

They tell me you are wicked and I believe them, for I have seen your
    painted women under the gas lamps luring the farm boys.
And they tell me you are crooked and I answer: Yes, it is true I have
    seen the gunman kill and go free to kill again.
And they tell me you are brutal and my reply is: On the faces of women
    and children I have seen the marks of wanton hunger.
And having answered so I turn once more to those who sneer at this
    my city, and I give them back the sneer and say to them:
Come and show me another city with lifted head singing so proud to
    be alive and coarse and strong and cunning.
Flinging magnetic curses amid the toil of piling job on job, here is a
    tall bold slugger set vivid against the little soft cities;
Fierce as a dog with tongue lapping for action, cunning as a savage
    pitted against the wilderness,

Bareheaded,
Shoveling,
Wrecking,
Planning,
Building, breaking, rebuilding,
Under the smoke, dust all over his mouth, laughing with white teeth,
Under the terrible burden of destiny laughing as a young man laughs,
Laughing even as an ignorant fighter laughs who has never lost a battle,
Bragging and laughing that under his wrist is the pulse, and under his
   ribs the heart of the people,
                Laughing!
Laughing the stormy, husky, brawling laughter of Youth, half-naked,
   sweating, proud to be Hog Butcher, Tool Maker, Stacker of Wheat,
   Player with Railroads and Freight Handler to the Nation.

Excerpt from "Prairie"

I was born on the prairie, and the milk of its wheat,
   the red of its clover, the eyes of its women, gave me a
   song and a slogan.

Here, the water went down, the icebergs slid with gravel,
   the gaps and the valleys hissed, and the black loam came,
   and the yellow sandy loam.

Here between the shreds of the Rocky Mountains and the
   Appalachians, here now a morning-star fixes a fire sign
   over the timber claims and cow pastures, the corn belt,
   the cotton belt, the cattle ranches.

Here the grey geese go five hundred miles and back with a
   wind under their wings, honking the cry for a new home.

Here I know I will hanker after nothing so much as one
   more sunrise, or a sky moon of fire doubled to a river
   moon of water.

Excerpt from "The People, Yes"

Lincoln?
He was a mystery in smoke and flags
Saying yes to the smoke, yes to the flags,
Yes to the paradoxes of democracy,
Yes to the hopes of government

Of the people by the people for the people,
No to debauchery of the public mind,
No to personal malice nursed and fed,
Yes to the Constitution when a help,
No to the Constitution when a hindrance
Yes to man as a struggler amid illusions,
Each man fated to answer for himself:
Which of the faiths and illusions of mankind
Must I choose for my own sustaining light
To bring me beyond the present wilderness?

    Lincoln? Was he a poet?
    And did he write verses?
"I have not willingly planted a thorn
    in any man's bosom."
I shall do nothing through malice: what
    I deal with is too vast for malice."

Death was in the air.
So was birth.
What was dying few could say.
What was being born none could know.

GEORGE M. COHAN (1878–1942)

An actor, songwriter, playwright, and producer, Cohan wrote "You're a Grand Old Flag" for the first act of his 1906 stage musical, *George Washington, Jr.* It was the first song from a musical to sell over a million copies of sheet music. Cohan also wrote the popular WWI-era song, "Over There," for which he received the U.S. Congressional Medal of Honor. *Yankee Doodle Dandy*, a biographical musical film about Cohan starring James Cagney, takes its title from the celebrated, and irreverent, Cohan song "The Yankee Doodle Boy."

The Yankee Doodle Boy

I'm the kid that's all the candy,
I'm a Yankee Doodle Dandy,
I'm glad I am,
(So's Uncle Sam.)

I'm a real live Yankee Doodle,
Made my name and fame and boodle,
Just like Mister Doodle did, by riding on a pony.
I love to listen to the Dixie strain,
"I long to see the girl I left behind me;"
And that ain't a josh,
She's a Yankee, by gosh.
(Oh, say can you see,
Anything about a Yankee that's a phony?)

Chorus:
I'm a Yankee Doodle Dandy,
A Yankee Doodle, do or die;
A real live nephew of my Uncle Sam's,
Born on the Fourth of July.
I've got a Yankee Doodle sweetheart,
She's my Yankee Doodle joy.
Yankee Doodle came to London,
Just to ride the ponies;
I am the Yankee Doodle Boy.

Father's name was Hezikiah,
Mother's name was Ann Maria,
Yanks through and through.
(Red, white, and blue.)
Father was so Yankee-hearted,
When the Spanish war was started,
He slipped on his uniform and hopped upon a pony.
My mother's mother was a Yankee true,
My father's father was Yankee too:
And that's going some,
For the Yankees, by gum.
(Oh, say can you see
Anything about my pedigree that's phony?)

You're a Grand Old Flag

There's a feeling comes a-stealing and it sets my brain a-reeling,
When I'm list'ning to the music of a military band.
Any tune like "Yankee Doodle" simply sets me off my noodle,
It's that patriotic something that no one can understand.

"Way down south, in the land of cotton," melody untiring,
Ain't that inspiring!
Hurrah! Hurrah! We'll join the jubilee!
And that's going some for the Yankees, by gum!
Red, White and Blue,
I am for you.
Honest, you're a grand old flag.

Chorus:
You're a grand old flag, You're a high-flying flag,
And forever in peace may you wave.
You're the emblem of the land I love,
The home of the free and the brave.
Ev'ry heart beats true under Red, White and Blue,
Where there's never a boast or brag;
"But should auld acquaintance be forgot,"
Keep your eye on the grand old flag.

I'm a cranky, hanky panky, I'm a dead-square, honest Yankee,
And I'm mighty proud of that old flag that flies for Uncle Sam.
Though I don't believe in raving ev'ry time I see it waving,
There's a chill runs up my back that makes me glad I'm what I am.
Here's a land with a million soldiers, that's if we should need 'em,
We'll fight for freedom!
Hurrah! Hurrah! For ev'ry Yankee tar
And old G.A.R., ev'ry stripe, ev'ry star.
Red, White and Blue,
Hats off to you,
Honest, you're a grand old flag.

VACHEL LINDSAY (1879–1931)

Lindsay spent time wandering throughout the Midwest reciting his poems in exchange for food and shelter. In part, his readings were an effort to keep poetry alive as an oral form. Lindsay was born in a house where Abraham Lincoln's sister-in-law had once lived; the poet was aware that Lincoln had visited the house several times.

Lincoln

Would I might rouse the Lincoln in you all,
That which is gendered in the wilderness
From lonely prairies and God's tenderness.
Imperial soul, star of a weedy stream,
Born where the ghosts of buffaloes still dream,
Whose spirit hoof-beats storm above his grave,
Above that breast of earth and prairie-fire—
Fire that freed the slave.

Abraham Lincoln Walks at Midnight

(In Springfield, Illinois)

It is portentous, and a thing of state
That here at midnight, in our little town
A mourning figure walks, and will not rest,
Near the old court-house pacing up and down.

Or by his homestead, or in shadowed yards
He lingers where his children used to play,
Or through the market, on the well-worn stones
He stalks until the dawn-stars burn away.

A bronzed, lank man! His suit of ancient black,
A famous high top-hat and plain worn shawl
Make him the quaint great figure that men love,
The prairie-lawyer, master of us all.

He cannot sleep upon his hillside now.
He is among us:—as in times before!
And we who toss and lie awake for long
Breathe deep, and start, to see him pass the door.

His head is bowed. He thinks on men and kings.
Yea, when the sick world cries, how can he sleep?
Too many peasants fight, they know not why,
Too many homesteads in black terror weep.

The sins of all the war-lords burn his heart.
He sees the dreadnaughts scouring every main.
He carries on his shawl-wrapped shoulders now
The bitterness, the folly and the pain.

He cannot rest until a spirit-dawn
Shall come;—the shining hope of Europe free;
The league of sober folk, the Workers' Earth,
Bringing long peace to Cornland, Alp and Sea.

It breaks his heart that kings must murder still,
That all his hours of travail here for men
Seem yet in vain. And who will bring white peace
That he may sleep upon his hill again?

Why I Voted the Socialist Ticket

I am unjust, but I can strive for justice.
My life's unkind, but I can vote for kindness.
I, the unloving, say life should be lovely.
I, that am blind, cry out against my blindness.

Man is a curious brute—he pets his fancies—
Fighting mankind, to win sweet luxury.
So he will be, though law be clear as crystal,
Tho' all men plan to live in harmony.

Come, let us vote against our human nature,
Crying to God in all the polling places
To heal our everlasting sinfulness
And make us sages with transfigured faces.

EDWARD SMYTH JONES (1881–1968)

In 1910, Jones walked from Indianapolis, Indiana, to Cambridge, Massachusetts, in the hope of finding work and furthering his education, perhaps at Harvard. He was arrested for vagrancy, but when the judge read a poem Jones wrote in jail called "Harvard Square," the African American poet was released. Two years later, when Jones was profiled in the *New York Times*, he was working as a waiter at the Faculty Club of Columbia University in New York City. Jones dedicated a book of poems, *The Sylvan Cabin*, to the judge who freed him.

Flag of the Free

Flag of the free, our sable sires
  First bore thee long ago
Into hot battles' hell-lit fires,
  Against the fiercest foe.
And when he shook his shaggy mien,
  And made the death-knell ring,
Brave Attucks fell upon the Green,
  Thy stripes first crimsoning!

Thy might and majesty we hurl,
  Against the bolts of Mars,
And from thy ample folds unfurl
  Thy field of flaming stars!
Fond hope to nations in distress,
  Thy starry gleam shall give;
The stricken in the wilderness
  Shall look to thee and live.

What matter if where Boreas roars,
  Or where sweet Zephyr smiles?
What matter it where eagle soars,
  Or in the sunlit isles;
The flowing crimson stripes shall wave
  Above the bluish brine,
Emblazoned ensign of the brave,
  And Liberty enshrine!

Flag of the Free, still float on high
  Through every age to come;
Bright beacon of the azure sky,
  True light of Freedom's dome.

Till nations all shall cease to grope
    In vain for liberty,
O shine, last lingering star of hope
    Of all humanity!

A Song of Thanks

For the sun that shone at the dawn of spring,
For the flowers which bloom and the birds that sing,
For the verdant robe of the gray old earth,
For her coffers filled with their countless worth,
For the flocks which feed on a thousand hills,
For the rippling streams which turn the mills,
For the lowing herds in the lovely vale,
For the songs of gladness on the gale,—
From the Gulf and the Lakes to the Oceans' banks,—
Lord God of Hosts, we give Thee thanks!

For the farmer reaping his whitened fields,
For the bounty which the rich soil yields,
For the cooling dews and refreshing rains,
For the sun which ripens the golden grains,
For the bearded wheat and the fattened swine,
For the stallèd ox and the fruitful vine,
For the tubers large and cotton white,
For the kid and the lambkin frisk and blithe,
For the swan which floats near the river-banks,—
Lord God of Hosts, we give Thee thanks!

For the pumpkin sweet and the yellow yam,
For the corn and beans and the sugared ham,
For the plum and the peach and the apple red,
For the dear old press where the wine is tread,
For the cock which crows at the breaking dawn,
And the proud old "turk" of the farmer's barn,
For the fish which swim in the babbling brooks,
For the game which hide in the shady nooks,—
From the Gulf and the Lakes to the Oceans' banks—
Lord God of Hosts, we give Thee thanks!

For the sturdy oaks and the stately pines,
For the lead and the coal from the deep, dark mines,
For the silver ores of a thousand fold,
For the diamond bright and the yellow gold,
For the river boat and the flying train,
For the fleecy sail of the rolling main,
For the velvet sponge and the glossy pearl,
For the flag of peace which we now unfurl,—
From the Gulf and the Lakes to the Oceans' banks,—
Lord God of Hosts, we give Thee thanks!

For the lowly cot and the mansion fair,
For the peace and plenty together share,
For the Hand which guides us from above,
For Thy tender mercies, abiding love,
For the blessed home with its children gay,
For returnings of Thanksgiving Day,
For the bearing toils and the sharing cares,
We lift up our hearts in our songs and our prayers,—
From the Gulf and the Lakes to the Oceans' banks,—
Lord God of Hosts, we give Thee thanks!

JOHN GOULD FLETCHER (1886–1950)

An Arkansas native, Fletcher spent part of his life in England, where he was associated with Imagist poets Ezra Pound and Amy Lowell. After returning to the United States, he became active with a group of writers called the Southern Agrarians. He won the Pulitzer Prize in Poetry in 1939 for *Selected Poems*.

Lincoln

I

Like a gaunt, scraggly pine
Which lifts its head above the mournful sandhills;
And patiently, through dull years of bitter silence,
Untended and uncared for, begins to grow.

Ungainly, labouring, huge,
The wind of the north has twisted and gnarled its branches;
Yet in the heat of midsummer days, when thunder-clouds ring the
    horizon,
A nation of men shall rest beneath its shade.

And it shall protect them all,
Hold everyone safe there, watching aloof in silence;
Until at last one mad stray bolt from the zenith
Shall strike it in an instant down to earth.

II

There was a darkness in this man; an immense and hollow darkness,
Of which we may not speak, nor share with him, nor enter;
A darkness through which strong roots stretched downwards into the
    earth
Towards old things;
Towards the herdman-kings who walked the earth and spoke with
    God,
Towards the wanderers who sought for they knew not what, and found
    their goal at last;
Towards the men who waited, only waited patiently when all seemed
    lost,
Many bitter winters of defeat;
Down to the granite of patience
These roots swept, knotted fibrous roots, prying, piercing, seeking,
And drew from the living rock and the living waters about it
The red sap to carry upwards to the sun.

Not proud, but humble,
Only to serve and pass on, to endure to the end through service;
For the ax is laid at the root of the trees, and all that bring not forth
    good fruit
Shall be cut down on the day to come and cast into the fire.

III

There is silence abroad in the land to-day,
And in the hearts of men, a deep and anxious silence;
And, because we are still at last, those bronze lips slowly open,
Those hollow and weary eyes take on a gleam of light.

Slowly a patient, firm-syllabled voice cuts through the endless silence
Like labouring oxen that drag a plow through the chaos of rude clay-
    fields:
"I went forward as the light goes forward in early spring,
But there were also many things which I left behind.

"Tombs that were quiet;
One, of a mother, whose brief light went out in the darkness,
One, of a loved one, the snow on whose grave is long falling,
One, only of a child, but it was mine.

"Have you forgot your graves? Go, question them in anguish,
Listen long to their unstirred lips. From your hostages to silence,
Learn there is no life without death, no dawn without sun-setting,
No victory but to Him who has given all."

IV

The clamour of cannon dies down, the furnace-mouth of the battle is
    silent.
The midwinter sun dips and descends, the earth takes on afresh its
    bright colours.
But he whom we mocked and obeyed not, he whom we scorned and
    mistrusted,
He has descended, like a god, to his rest.

Over the uproar of cities,
Over the million intricate threads of life wavering and crossing,
In the midst of problems we know not, tangling, perplexing, ensnaring,
Rises one white tomb alone.

Beam over it, stars.
Wrap it round, stripes—stripes red for the pain that he bore for you—
Enfold it forever, O flag, rent, soiled, but repaired through your anguish;
Long as you keep him there safe, the nations shall bow to your law.

Strew over him flowers;
Blue forget-me-nots from the north, and the bright pink arbutus
From the east, and from the west rich orange blossoms,
But from the heart of the land take the passion-flower.

Rayed, violet, dim,
With the nails that pierced, the cross that he bore and the circlet,
And beside it there, lay also one lonely snow-white magnolia,
Bitter for remembrance of the healing which has passed.

JOYCE KILMER (1886–1918)

Kilmer was a poet, editor, journalist, and lecturer before he enlisted in the
Army and died in battle at the Second Battle of the Marne in France during
WWI. Kilmer had written "Rouge Bouquet" four months earlier in honor
of fellow American soldiers who had died in an artillery barrage.

Rouge Bouquet

In a wood they call the Rouge Bouquet
    There is a new-made grave to-day,
Built by never a spade nor pick
Yet covered with earth ten metres thick.
There lie many fighting men,
    Dead in their youthful prime,
Never to laugh nor love again
    Nor taste the Summertime.
For Death came flying through the air
And stopped his flight at the dugout stair,
Touched his prey and left them there,
    Clay to clay.
He hid their bodies stealthily
In the soil of the land they fought to free
    And fled away.
Now over the grave abrupt and clear
    Three volleys ring;
And perhaps their brave young spirits hear
    The bugle sing:
"Go to sleep!
Go to sleep!
Slumber well where the shell screamed and fell.
Let your rifles rest on the muddy floor,

You will not need them any more.
Danger's past;
Now at last,
Go to sleep!"

There is on earth no worthier grave
To hold the bodies of the brave
Than this place of pain and pride
Where they nobly fought and nobly died.
Never fear but in the skies
Saints and angels stand
Smiling with their holy eyes
    On this new-come band.
St. Michael's sword darts through the air
And touches the aureole on his hair
As he sees them stand saluting there,
    His stalwart sons;
And Patrick, Brigid, Columkill
Rejoice that in veins of warriors still
    The Gael's blood runs.
And up to Heaven's doorway floats,
From the wood called Rouge Bouquet,
A delicate cloud of buglenotes
    That softly say:
"Farewell!
Farewell!
Comrades true, born anew, peace to you!
Your souls shall be where the heroes are
And your memory shine like the morning-star.
Brave and dear,
Shield us here.
Farewell!"

ROBINSON JEFFERS (1887–1962)

Living in semi-seclusion on the central coast of California, Jeffers wrote about the natural world and his beliefs about humanity. He is best known for his shorter, vivid verse about nature, poems that made him an early icon of the environmental movement.

Shine, Republic

The quality of these trees, green height; of the sky, shining, of water,
    a clear flow; of the rock, hardness
And reticence: each is noble in its quality. The love of freedom has
    been the quality of western man.

There is a stubborn torch that flames from Marathon to Concord, its
    dangerous beauty binding three ages
Into one time; the waves of barbarism and civilization have eclipsed
    but have never quenched it.

For the Greeks the love of beauty, for Rome of ruling; for the present
    age the passionate love of discovery;
But in one noble passion we are one; and Washington, Luther, Tacitus,
    Aeschylus, one kind of man.

And you, America, that passion made you. You were not born to
    prosperity, you were born to love freedom.
You did not say "en masse," you said "independence." But we cannot
    have all the luxuries and freedom also.

Freedom is poor and laborious; that torch is not safe but hungry, and
    often requires blood for its fuel.
You will tame it against it burn too clearly, you will hood it like a kept
    hawk, you will perch it on the wrist of Caesar.

But keep the tradition, conserve the forms, the observances, keep the
    spot sore. Be great, carve deep your heel-marks.
The states of the next age will no doubt remember you, and edge their
    love of freedom with contempt of luxury.

CLAUDE MCKAY (1890–1948)

A seminal member of the Harlem Renaissance, the Jamaican-born McKay's experience of American racism was often the topic of his writing. *Home to Harlem,* published in 1928, was the most popular novel written by a person of African ancestry to that date. McKay spent over a dozen years abroad before returning to America in 1934. He became a citizen in 1940.

America

Although she feeds me bread of bitterness,
And sinks into my throat her tiger's tooth,
Stealing my breath of life, I will confess
I love this cultured hell that tests my youth!
Her vigor flows like tides into my blood,
Giving me strength erect against her hate.
Her bigness sweeps my being like a flood.
Yet as a rebel fronts a king in state,
I stand within her walls with not a shred
Of terror, malice, not a word of jeer.
Darkly I gaze into the days ahead,
And see her might and granite wonders there,
Beneath the touch of Time's unerring hand,
Like priceless treasures sinking in the sand.

KATHERINE GARRISON CHAPIN BIDDLE (1890–1977)

Author, lecturer, and arts advocate Chapin was appointed one of the original Fellows in American Letters of the Library of Congress. Her poem "Plain-Chant for America" was set to music by composer William Grant Still; it was performed in 1941 by the New York Philharmonic in Carnegie Hall. Still dedicated the "Plain-Chant" score to Eleanor Roosevelt.

Plain-Chant for America

For the dream unfinished
Out of which we came,
We stand together,
While a hemisphere darkens
And the nations flame.

Our earth has been hallowed
With death for freedom;
Our walls have been hallowed
With freedom's thought.

Concord, Valley Forge, Harpers Ferry
Light up with their flares
Our sky of doubt.

We fear tyranny as our hidden enemy:
the black-shirt cruelty, the goose-step mind.

No dark signs close the doors of our speaking,
No bayonets bar the door to our prayers,
No gun butts shadow our children's eyes.

If we have failed—lynchings in Georgia,
Justice in Massachusetts undone,
The bloody fields of South Chicago—
Still a voice from the bruised and the battered
Speaks out in the light of a free sun.

Saying: "Tell them again, say it, America;
Say it again till it splits their ears:
Freedom is salt in our blood and its bone shape;
If freedom fails, we'll fight for more freedom—
This is the land, and these are the years!
When freedom's a whisper above their ashes
An obsolete word cut on their graves,
When the mind has yielded its last resistance,
And the last free flag is under the waves—
Let them remember that here on the western
Horizon a star, once acclaimed, has not set;
And the strength of a hope, and the shape of a vision
Died for and sung for and fought for,
And worked for,
Is living yet."

JOSEPH SEAMON COTTER, JR.
(1895–1919)

Cotter's father, also a poet, was the principal and founder of the Paul Laurence Dunbar School in Louisville, Kentucky. Cotter attended Fisk University but had to drop out when he became ill with tuberculosis. He died at the age of twenty-three.

A Sonnet to Negro Soldiers
(Dedicated to the Ninety-Second Division,
U.S. National Army)

They shall go down unto Life's Borderland,
    Walk unafraid within that Living Hell,
      Nor heed the driving rain of shot and shell
That 'round them falls; but with uplifted hand
Be one with mighty hosts, an armed band
    Against man's wrong to man—for such full well
      They know. And from their trembling lips shall swell
A song of hope the world can understand.

All this to them shall be a glorious sign,
    A glimmer of that Resurrection Morn,
When age-long Faith, crowned with a grace benign,
    Shall rise and from their blows cast down the thorn
Of Prejudice. E'en though through blood it be,
There breaks this day their dawn of Liberty.

STEPHEN VINCENT BENÉT (1898–1943)

In 1929, Benét received the Pulitzer Prize in Poetry for "John Brown's Body," his long narrative poem on the Civil War. Almost twenty-five years later, and ten years after the author had died, actor Charles Laughton performed a dramatization of the poem throughout the United States.

"John Brown's Body—Invocation"

American muse, whose strong and diverse heart
So many men have tried to understand
But only made it smaller with their art,
Because you are as various as your land,

As mountainous-deep, as flowered with blue rivers,
Thirsty with deserts, buried under snows,
As native as the shape of Navajo quivers,
And native, too, as the sea-voyaged rose.

Swift runner, never captured or subdued,
Seven-branched elk beside the mountain stream,
That half a hundred hunters have pursued
But never matched their bullets with the dream,

Where the great huntsmen failed, I set my sorry
And mortal snare for your immortal quarry.

You are the buffalo-ghost, the broncho-ghost
With dollar-silver in your saddle-horn,
The cowboys riding in from Painted Post,
The Indian arrow in the Indian corn,

And you are the clipped velvet of the lawns
Where Shropshire grows from Massachusetts sods,
The grey Maine rocks—and the war-painted dawns
That break above the Garden of the Gods.

The prairie-schooners crawling toward the ore
And the cheap car, parked by the station-door.

Where the skyscrapers lift their foggy plumes
Of stranded smoke out of a stony mouth
You are that high stone and its arrogant fumes,
And you are ruined gardens in the South

And bleak New England farms, so winter-white
Even their roofs look lonely, and the deep
The middle grainland where the wind of night
Is like all blind earth sighing in her sleep.

A friend, an enemy, a sacred hag
With two tied oceans in her medicine-bag.

They tried to fit you with an English song
And clip your speech into the English tale.
But, even from the first, the words went wrong,
The catbird pecked away the nightingale.

The homesick men begot high-cheekboned things
Whose wit was whittled with a different sound
And Thames and all the rivers of the kings
Ran into Mississippi and were drowned.

They planted England with a stubborn trust.
But the cleft dust was never English dust.

Stepchild of every exile from content
And all the disavouched, hard-bitten pack
Shipped overseas to steal a continent
With neither shirts nor honor to their back.

Pimping grandee and rump-faced regicide,
Apple-cheeked younkers from a windmill-square,
Puritans stubborn as the nails of Pride,
Rakes from Versailles and thieves from County Clare,

The black-robed priests who broke their hearts in vain
To make you God and France or God and Spain.

These were your lovers in your buckskin-youth.
And each one married with a dream so proud
He never knew it could not be the truth
And that he coupled with a girl of cloud.

And now to see you is more difficult yet
Except as an immensity of wheel
Made up of wheels, oiled with inhuman sweat
And glittering with the heat of ladled steel.

All these you are, and each is partly you,
And none is false, and none is wholly true.

So how to see you as you really are,
So how to suck the pure, distillate, stored
Essence of essence from the hidden star
And make it pierce like a riposting sword.

For, as we hunt you down, you must escape
And we pursue a shadow of our own
That can be caught in a magician's cape
But has the flatness of a painted stone.

Never the running stag, the gull at wing,
The pure elixir, the American thing.

And yet, at moments when the mind was hot
With something fierier than joy or grief,
When each known spot was an eternal spot
And every leaf was an immortal leaf,

I think that I have seen you, not as one,
But clad in diverse semblances and powers,
Always the same, as light falls from the sun,
And always different, as the differing hours.

Yet, through each altered garment that you wore,
The naked body, shaking the heart's core.

All day the snow fell on that Eastern town
With its soft, pelting, little, endless sigh
Of infinite flakes that brought the tall sky down
Till I could put my hands in the white sky

And taste cold scraps of heaven on my tongue
And walk in such a changed and luminous light
As gods inhabit when the gods are young.
All day it fell. And when the gathered night

Was a blue shadow cast by a pale glow
I saw you then, snow-image, bird of the snow.

And I have seen and heard you in the dry
Close-huddled furnace of the city street
When the parched moon was planted in the sky
And the limp air hung dead against the heat.

I saw you rise, red as that rusty plant,
Dizzied with lights, half-mad with senseless sound,
Enormous metal, shaking to the chant
Of a triphammer striking iron ground.

Enormous power, ugly to the fool,
And beautiful as a well-handled tool.

These, and the memory of that windy day
On the bare hills, beyond the last barbed wire,
When all the orange poppies bloomed one way
As if a breath would blow them into fire,

I keep forever, like the sea-lion's tusk
The broken sailor brings away to land,
But when he touches it, he smells the musk,
And the whole sea lies hollow in his hand.

So, from a hundred visions, I make one,
And out of darkness build my mocking sun.

And should that task seem fruitless in the eyes
Of those a different magic sets apart
To see through the ice-crystal of the wise
No nation but the nation that is Art,

Their words are just. But when the birchbark-call
Is shaken with the sound that hunters make
The moose comes plunging through the forest-wall
Although the rifle waits beside the lake.

Art has no nations—but the mortal sky
Lingers like gold in immortality.

This flesh was seeded from no foreign grain
But Pennsylvania and Kentucky wheat,
And it has soaked in California rain
And five years tempered in New England sleet

To strive at last, against an alien proof
And by the changes of an alien moon,
To build again that blue, American roof
Over a half-forgotten battle-tune

And call unsurely, from a haunted ground,
Armies of shadows and the shadow-sound.

In your Long House there is an attic-place
Full of dead epics and machines that rust,
And there, occasionally, with casual face,
You come awhile to stir the sleepy dust;

Neither in pride nor mercy, but in vast
Indifference at so many gifts unsought,
The yellowed satins, smelling of the past,
And all the loot the lucky pirates brought.

I only bring a cup of silver air,
Yet, in your casualness, receive it there.

Receive the dream too haughty for the breast,
Receive the words that should have walked as bold
As the storm walks along the mountain-crest
And are like beggars whining in the cold.

The maimed presumption, the unskilful skill,
The patchwork colors, fading from the first,
And all the fire that fretted at the will
With such a barren ecstasy of thirst.

Receive them all—and should you choose to touch them
With one slant ray of quick, American light,
Even the dust will have no power to smutch them,
Even the worst will glitter in the night.

If not—the dry bones littered by the way
May still point giants toward their golden prey.

LANGSTON HUGHES (1902–1967)

Hughes wrote one of his most famous poems, "The Negro Speaks of Rivers,"
during the summer after he graduated from high school. In his poems, stories,
and plays, Hughes addressed the complexity of urban African American life
in the United States during the early and mid-twentieth century: its horrors
and injustices as well as vibrancy and grace. He was a seminal member of the
Harlem Renaissance.

I, Too

I, too, sing America.

I am the darker brother.
They send me to eat in the kitchen
When company comes,

But I laugh,
And eat well,
And grow strong.

Tomorrow,
I'll be at the table
When company comes.
Nobody'll dare
Say to me,
"Eat in the kitchen,"
Then.

Besides,
They'll see how beautiful I am
And be ashamed—

I, too, am America.

Let America Be America Again

Let America be America again.
Let it be the dream it used to be.
Let it be the pioneer on the plain
Seeking a a home where he himself is free.

(America never was America to me.)

Let America be the dream the dreamers dreamed—
Let it be that great strong land of love
Where never kings connive nor tyrants scheme
That any man be crushed by one above.

(It never was America to me.)

O, let my land be a land where Liberty
Is crowned with no false patriotic wreath,
But opportunity is real, and life is free,
Equality is in the air we breathe.

(There's never been equality for me,
Nor freedom in this "homeland of the free.")

Say, who are you that mumbles in the dark?
And who are you that draws your veil across the stars?

I am the poor white, fooled and pushed apart,
I am the Negro bearing slavery's scars.
I am the red man driven from the land,
I am the immigrant clutching the hope I seek—
And finding only the same old stupid plan
Of dog eat dog, of mighty crush the weak.

I am the young man, full of strength and hope,
Tangled in that ancient endless chain
Of profit, power, gain, of grab the land!
Of grab the gold! Of grab the ways of satisfying need!
Of work the men! Of take the pay!
Of owning everything for one's own greed!

I am the farmer, bondsman to the soil.
I am the worker sold to the machine.
I am the Negro, servant to you all.
I am the people, humble, hungry, mean—
Hungry yet today despite the dream.
Beaten yet today—O, Pioneers!
I am the man who never got ahead,
The poorest worker bartered through the years.

Yet I'm the one who dreamt our basic dream
In the Old World while still a serf of kings,
Who dreamt a dream so strong, so brave, so true,
That even yet its might daring sings
In every brick and stone, in every furrow turned
That's made America the land it has become.
O, I'm the man who sailed those early seas
In search of what I meant to be my home—
For I'm the one who left dark Ireland's shore,
And Poland's plain, and England's grassy lea,
And torn from Black Africa's strand I came
To build a "homeland of the free."

The free?

Who said the free? Not me?
Surely not me? The millions on relief today?
The millions shot down when we strike?
The millions who have nothing for our pay?
For all the dreams we've dreamed

And all the songs we've sung
And all the hopes we've held
And all the flags we've hung,
The millions who have nothing for our pay—
Except the dream that's almost dead today.

O, let America be America again—
The land that never has been yet—
And yet must be—the land where every man is free.
The land that's mine—the poor man's, Indian's, Negro's,
ME—
Who made America,
Whose sweat and blood, whose faith and pain,
Whose hand at the foundry, whose plow in the rain,
Must bring back our mighty dream again.

Sure, call me any ugly name you choose—
The steel of freedom does not stain.
From those who live like leeches on the people's lives,
We must take back our land again,
America!

O, yes,
I say it plain,
America never was America to me,
And yet I swear this oath—
America will be!

Out of the rack and ruin of our gangster death,
The rape and rot of graft, and stealth, and lies,
We, the people, must redeem
The land, the mines, the plants, the rivers.
The mountains and the endless plain—
All, all the stretch of these great green states—
And make America again!

Daybreak in Alabama

When I get to be a composer
I'm gonna write me some music about
Daybreak in Alabama
And I'm gonna put the purtiest songs in it

Rising out of the ground like a swamp mist
And falling out of heaven like soft dew.
I'm gonna put some tall tall trees in it
And the scent of pine needles
And the smell of red clay after rain
And long red necks
And poppy colored faces
And big brown arms
And the field daisy eyes
Of black and white black white black people
And I'm gonna put white hands
And black hands and brown and yellow hands
And red clay earth hands in it
Touching everybody with kind fingers
And touching each other natural as dew
In that dawn of music when I
Get to be a composer
And write about daybreak
In Alabama.

WOODY GUTHRIE (1912–1967)

Named by his father after President Woodrow Wilson, Guthrie was a song-writer and folksinger from Oklahoma who chronicled the plight of the common American during the Great Depression and the decades that followed. His politically charged songs inspired the folk-music revival in the 1960s.

This Land Is Your Land

This land is your land, this land is my land
From California to the New York island;
From the redwood forest to the Gulf Stream waters
This land was made for you and me.

As I was walking that ribbon of highway,
I saw above me that endless skyway:
I saw below me that golden valley:
This land was made for you and me.

I've roamed and rambled and I followed my footsteps
To the sparkling sands of her diamond deserts;
And all around me a voice was sounding:
This land was made for you and me.

When the sun came shining, and I was strolling,
And the wheat fields waving and the dust clouds rolling,
As the fog was lifting a voice was chanting:
This land was made for you and me.

As I went walking I saw a sign there
And on the sign it said, "No Trespassing."
But on the other side it didn't say nothing,
That side was made for you and me.

In the shadow of the steeple I saw my people,
By the relief office I seen my people;
As they stood there hungry, I stood there asking
Is this land made for you and me?

Nobody living can ever stop me,
As I go walking that freedom highway;
Nobody living can ever make me turn back
This land was made for you and me.

LAWRENCE FERLINGHETTI (b. 1919)

A poet, playwright, publisher, artist, and activist, Ferlinghetti was at the forefront of San Francisco's literary renaissance of the 1950s and a West Coast associate of the "Beat" poets in New York City. He was the co-founder, along with Peter D. Martin, of City Lights Bookstore, the first all-paperback bookshop in the United States. After the departure of Martin, Ferlinghetti launched the publishing arm of City Lights, which went on to publish domestic and international authors of all genres.

I Am Waiting

I am waiting for my case to come up
and I am waiting
for a rebirth of wonder
and I am waiting for someone

to really discover America
and wail
and I am waiting
for the discovery
of a new symbolic western frontier
and I am waiting
for the American Eagle
to really spread its wings
and straighten up and fly right
and I am waiting
for the Age of Anxiety
to drop dead
and I am waiting
for the war to be fought
which will make the world safe
for anarchy
and I am waiting
for the final withering away
of all governments
and I am perpetually awaiting
a rebirth of wonder

I am waiting for the Second Coming
and I am waiting
for a religious revival
to sweep thru the state of Arizona
and I am waiting
for the Grapes of Wrath to be stored
and I am waiting
for them to prove
that God is really American
and I am waiting
to see God on television
piped onto church altars
if only they can find
the right channel
to tune in on
and I am waiting
for the Last Supper to be served again
with a strange new appetizer
and I am perpetually awaiting
a rebirth of wonder

I am waiting for my number to be called
and I am waiting
for the Salvation Army to take over
and I am waiting
for the meek to be blessed
and inherit the earth
without taxes
and I am waiting
for forests and animals
to reclaim the earth as theirs
and I am waiting
for a way to be devised
to destroy all nationalisms
without killing anybody
and I am waiting
for linnets and planets to fall like rain
and I am waiting for lovers and weepers
to lie down together again
in a new rebirth of wonder

I am waiting for the Great Divide to be crossed
and I am anxiously waiting
for the secret of eternal life to be discovered
by an obscure general practitioner
and I am waiting
for the storms of life
to be over
and I am waiting
to set sail for happiness
and I am waiting
for a reconstructed Mayflower
to reach America
with its picture story and tv rights
sold in advance to the natives
and I am waiting
for the lost music to sound again
in the Lost Continent
in a new rebirth of wonder

I am waiting for the day
that maketh all things clear
and I am awaiting retribution
for what America did
to Tom Sawyer
and I am waiting
for Alice in Wonderland
to retransmit to me
her total dream of innocence
and I am waiting
for Childe Roland to come
to the final darkest tower
and I am waiting
for Aphrodite
to grow live arms
at a final disarmament conference
in a new rebirth of wonder

I am waiting
to get some intimations
of immortality
by recollecting my early childhood
and I am waiting
for the green mornings to come again
youth's dumb green fields come back again
and I am waiting
for some strains of unpremeditated art
to shake my typewriter
and I am waiting to write
the great indelible poem
and I am waiting
for the last long careless rapture
and I am perpetually waiting
for the fleeing lovers on the Grecian Urn
to catch each other up at last
and embrace
and I am awaiting
perpetually and forever
a renaissance of wonder

MAYA ANGELOU (1928–2014)

Angelou was an author, educator, actress, director, producer, historian, and civil rights activist. In addition to receiving numerous degrees, fellowships, prizes, and appointments, she was awarded the Presidential Medal of Arts in 2000 and the Lincoln Medal in 2008. Her poem "On the Pulse of Morning" was written for the inauguration of the forty-second president of the United States, William Jefferson Clinton.

Excerpt from "On the Pulse of Morning"

You, who gave me my first name, you
Pawnee, Apache, Seneca, you
Cherokee Nation, who rested with me, then
Forced on bloody feet, left me to the employment of
Other seekers—desperate for gain,
Starving for gold.
You, the Turk, the Swede, the German, the Eskimo, the Scot ...
You the Ashanti, the Yoruba, the Kru, bought
Sold, stolen, arriving on a nightmare
Praying for a dream.
Here, root yourselves beside me.
I am that Tree planted by the River,
Which will not be moved.
I, the Rock, I the River, I the Tree
I am yours—your Passages have been paid.
Lift up your faces, you have a piercing need
For this bright morning dawning for you.
History, despite its wrenching pain,
Cannot be unlived, but if faced
With courage, need not be lived again.
Lift up your eyes upon
This day breaking for you.

MYRA SKLAREW (b. 1934)

Former president of Yaddo Artists Community, Professor Emerita, American University and founder of the MFA Program in Creative Writing, Myra Sklarew has published 17 books, including poetry, fiction, and essays. Forthcoming is *A Survivor Named Trauma*, SUNY Press. "Monuments" was performed at the Kennedy Center for the Performing Arts in celebration of Washington, D.C. and the millennium.

Monuments

Today the moon sees fit to come between a parched earth
and sun, hurrying the premature darkness. A rooster in the yard
   cuts off its crowing, fooled into momentary sleep.
     And soon the Perseid showers, broken bits
of the ancient universe, will pass through the skin of our
   atmosphere. Time and space are alive over our city.

Final eclipse of the sun, last of this millennium, our city's
   brightness broken off. We have known other dark hours:
     Here, coffin that slowly passes, I give you my sprig
of lilac—Lincoln's death, winding procession toward sleep.
   We have known slave coffles and holding pens in yards
not half a mile from our Capitol, wooden palings sunk in earth

to guarantee none would escape. In this freest city. O if earth
   could talk. Earth does talk in the neatly framed yards
   where death thinks to lay us down to rest. Asleep,
   the marker stones. But not the voices, jagged bits
   of memory, shards of poems. Sterling Brown. Our
human possessions and all they've left us. This whole city

   sings their songs. Say *their* names. In this city
they are our monuments: Frederick Douglass, our
Rayford Logan, Alain Locke, Franklin Frazier, Georgia
Douglas Johnson, Paul Laurence Dunbar, May Miller. Not sleep
but garlands left to us. Montague Cobb, William Hastie. Yards
   of names. And here, the place where we unearth

   an immigrant father of seven. He leans down—no earthly
reason for his choice—to pick up his nearest child. A yard-long
   rack of brooms behind him, a bin of apples. Not the sleep
   of cold, but autumn in Washington. 1913 or a bit

later. He stands awkwardly on 4 1/2 Street, S. W. Our
street photographer, who's just come by with his city

   chatter, ducks beneath a dark cloth. Monuments of the city
 behind him, he leans over his black box camera in time to capture
       that moment when the child will play her bit
part, pushing away from her father like a boat from shore. In the sleep
 of winter, years later, she will become my mother. What yardstick
     by which to measure importance? To measure earthly

agency? Each of us has monuments in the bone case of memory. Earth-
bound, I carry my sac of marble down lonely city streets where our
statues and a tall bearded man keep watch over all their citizens.

SHIRLEY GEOK-LIN LIM (b. 1944)

Born in Malacca, Malaysia, Lim spoke Malay and the Hokkin dialect of Chinese
before learning to read English at age six at a missionary school. In 1969, she
moved to the United States under a Fulbright scholarship to attend graduate
school at Brandeis University in Waltham, Massachusetts. She eventually
settled in Santa Barbara, California, where she is a professor in the English
department at the university there. In 1997, Lin won the American Book
Award for *Among the White Moon Faces: An Asian-American Memoir of Homelands*.

Learning to Love America

because it has no pure products

because the Pacific Ocean sweeps along the coastline
because the water of the ocean is cold
and because land is better than ocean

because I say we rather than they

because I live in California
I have eaten fresh artichokes
and jacaranda bloom in April and May

because my senses have caught up with my body
my breath with the air it swallows
my hunger with my mouth

because I walk barefoot in my house

because I have nursed my son at my breast
because he is a strong American boy
because I have seen his eyes redden when he is asked who he is
because he answers I don't know

because to have a son is to have a country
because my son will bury me here
because countries are in our blood and we bleed them

because it is late and too late to change my mind
because it is time.

GREGORY DJANIKIAN (b. 1949)

Born in Alexandria, Egypt, Djanikian moved with his family at age eight to Williamsport, Pennsylvania. He is currently the Director of the Creative Writing Program at the University of Pennsylvania. Among the awards Djanikian has received are a National Endowment for the Arts fellowship, the Eunice Tietjens Prize from *Poetry* magazine, and the Anahid Literary Award from the Armenian Center of Columbia University.

Sailing to America

Alexandria, 1956

The rugs had been rolled up and islands of them
Floated in the centers of every room,
And now, on the bare wood floors,
My sister and I were skimming among them
In the boats we'd made from newspaper,
Sheets of them pinned to each other,
Dhows, gondolas, clippers, arks.
There was a mule outside on the street
Braying under a load of figs, though mostly
There was quiet, a wind from the desert
Was putting the city to sleep,
But we were too far adrift, the air
Was scurfy and wet, the currents tricking

Our bows against reef and coral
And hulls shearing under the weight of cargo.
"Ahoy and belay!" I called to my sister,
"Avast, avast!" she yelled back from her rigging,
And neither of us knew what we were saying
But the words came to us as from a movie,
Cinemascopic, American. "Richard Widmark,"
I said. "Clark Gable, Bogie," she said,
"Yo-ho-ho." We had passed Cyprus
And now there was Crete or Sardinia
Maybe something larger further off.
The horizon was everywhere I turned,
The waters were becoming turgid,
They were roiling, weeks had passed.
"America, America, land-ho!" I yelled directionless.
"Gibraltar," my sister said, "Heave to,"
And signalling a right, her arm straight out,
She turned and bravely set our course
North-by-northwest for the New World.
Did we arrive? Years later, yes.
By plane, suddenly. With suitcases
And something as hazy as a future.
The November sun was pale and far off,
The air was colder than we'd ever felt,
And already these were wonders to us
As much as snow would be or evergreens,
And it would take me a long time
Before I'd ever remember
Boats made of paper, islands of wool,
And my sister's voice, as in a fog,
Calling out the hazards,
Leading me on, getting us there.

When I First Saw Snow

Tarrytown, N.Y.

Bing Crosby was singing "White Christmas"
    on the radio, we were staying at my aunt's house
      waiting for papers, my father was looking for a job.
We had trimmed the tree the night before,

sap had run on my fingers and for the first time
 I was smelling pine wherever I went.
Anais, my cousin, was upstairs in her room
 listening to Danny and the Juniors.
Haigo was playing Monopoly with Lucy, his sister,
 Buzzy, the boy next door, had eyes for her
 and there was a rattle of dice, a shuffling
 of Boardwalk, Park Place, Marvin Gardens.
There were red bows on the Christmas tree.
It had snowed all night.
My boot buckles were clinking like small bells
 as I thumped to the door and out
 onto the grey planks of the porch dusted with snow.
The world was immaculate, new,
 even the trees had changed color,
 and when I touched the snow on the railing
I didn't know what I had touched, ice or fire.
I heard, "I'm dreaming ..."
I heard, "At the hop, hop, hop ... oh, baby."
I heard "B & O" and the train in my imagination
 was whistling through the great plains.
And I was stepping off,
I was falling deeply into America.

Immigrant Picnic

It's the Fourth of July, the flags
are painting the town,
the plastic forks and knives
are laid out like a parade.

And I'm grilling, I've got my apron,
I've got potato salad, macaroni, relish,
I've got a hat shaped
like the state of Pennsylvania.

I ask my father what's his pleasure
and he says, "Hot dog, medium rare,"
and then, "Hamburger, sure,
what's the big difference,"
as if he's really asking.

I put on hamburgers and hot dogs,
slice up the sour pickles and Bermudas,
uncap the condiments. The paper napkins
are fluttering away like lost messages.

"You're running around," my mother says,
"like a chicken with its head loose."

"Ma," I say, "you mean cut off,
loose and cut off being as far apart
as, say, son and daughter."

She gives me a quizzical look as though
I've been caught in some impropriety.
"I love you and your sister just the same," she says,
"Sure," my grandmother pipes in,
"you're both our children, so why worry?"

That's not the point I begin telling them,
and I'm comparing words to fish now,
like the ones in the sea at Port Said,
or like birds among the date palms by the Nile,
unrepentantly elusive, wild.

"Sonia," my father says to my mother,
"what the hell is he talking about?"
"He's on a ball," my mother says.

"That's roll!" I say, throwing up my hands,
"as in hot dog, hamburger, dinner roll...."

"And what about roll out the barrels?" my mother asks,
and my father claps his hands, "Why sure," he says,
"let's have some fun," and launches
into a polka, twirling my mother
around and around like the happiest top,

and my uncle is shaking his head, saying
"You could grow nuts listening to us,"

and I'm thinking of pistachios in the Sinai
burgeoning without end,
pecans in the South, the jumbled
flavor of them suddenly in my mouth,
wordless, confusing,
crowding out everything else.

JULIA ALVAREZ (b. 1950)

A New York City native, Alvarez spent much of her youth in the Dominican
Republic. She explores her experience as a Dominican American in fiction
and essays as well as poems. Her novel *In the Time of the Butterflies* was adapted
into a 2001 feature film.

I, Too, Sing América

I know it's been said before
but not in this voice
of the plátano
and the mango,
marimba y bongó,
not in this sancocho
of inglés
con español.
Ay sí,
it's my turn
to oh say
what I see,
I'm going to sing America!
with all América
inside me:
from the soles
of Tierra del Fuego
to the thin waist
of Chiriquí
up the spine of the Mississippi
through the heartland
of the Yanquis

to the great plain face of Canada —
all of us
singing America,
the whole hemispheric
familia
belting our canción,
singing our brown skin
into that white
and red and blue song —
the big song
that sings
all America,
el canto
que cuenta
con toda América:
un *new song!*
Ya llegó el momento,
our moment
under the sun —
ese sol *that shines*
on everyone.
So, hit it maestro!
give us that Latin beat,
¡Uno-dos-tres!
One-two-three!
Ay sí,
(y bilingually):
Yo también soy América
I, too, am America.

Index of Titles

Index of First Lines